Richard Randolph

Sober Thoughts on Staple Themes

Richard Randolph

Sober Thoughts on Staple Themes

ISBN/EAN: 9783744652063

Printed in Europe, USA, Canada, Australia, Japan

Cover: Foto ©Thomas Meinert / pixelio.de

More available books at **www.hansebooks.com**

SOBER THOUGHTS

ON

STAPLE THEMES.

[*REVISED EDITION.*]

BY

RICHARD RANDOLPH,

AUTHOR OF "WINDFALLS," ETC.

" I simply state these propositions; I am not going to defend them. If they cannot defend tnemselves by the light which they throw on the anticipations and difficulties of the human spirit, by the hint of deliverance which they offer it, by the horrible dreams which they scatter, my arguments would be worth nothing."—F. D. MAURICE.

HENRY LONGSTRETH,

740 SANSOM STREET.

1889.

TO FAITHFUL WORKERS,

IN THE HOPE THAT, BENEATH THE TISSUE OF STUDIED WORDS
AND SENTENCES, THEY WILL FIND AN ESSENTIALLY UN-
PREMEDITATED LABOR OF LOVE, WITH RESULTS
OF THOUGHT WORTHY OF CANDID
CRITICISM IF NOT OF PRAC-
TICAL ADOPTION,

THESE PAGES ARE INSCRIBED.

SOBER THOUGHTS.

"THERE IS A SPIRITUAL BODY."

Oh, give me substance! is the cry
Methinks I hear, or see thee sigh,
Amused no more by idle toys,
Nor mocked with visionary joys.

The scenes which crowd thy mind's area,
Yield not the coveted idea
Of good triumphant o'er the grave,
And fitting for a soul to crave.

The senses, as the gates of mind,
The crumbling walls leave not behind;
And he who loiters at the gate
Must share the base partition's fate.

Partition-walls our bodies are,
The flow of Life Divine to bar,
Except we keep the sense-gates clear
For passage of the stream sincere.

The dome above rests not on them,
But on that Man of Bethlehem,
Whose body is the Christian's meat,
Whose soul sits on the mercy-seat.

Turn inward then thy spirit's eye,
And worship toward that inner sky
If thou wouldst gather light and strength
To range the temple's breadth and length!

The wonders of the holy church
Shall bountifully bless his search,
Whose cares of age or hopes of youth
Regard the Majesty of Truth.

CONTENTS.

SOBER THOUGHTS.

PROEM.

" In the world ye shall have tribulation, but be of good cheer : I have overcome the world.
—JOHN xvi. 33.

THE world hath served me well, I wot:
Not many as dark a dawn
Hath opened to a brighter lot,
As noon hath come and gone.

I may not hide it: gentle friends,
And life than early dreams
More fair, and work for cherished ends,
Are food for joy, me-seems.

But not in boasting would I sing!
My brother, who art thou,
That bendest to the gales which fling
Their fury on thee now?

I speak to thee.   Imagine not
That thou art all unknown,
And thine a solitary lot
With hope of succor flown!

A valley dark true souls must thread
On this side of the grave:
Turn thou from schemes and struggles dead,
To Him who waits to save!

Then to the bleak and gloomy day
　　Shall summer-light succeed,
And pleasant prospects by the way,
　　And strength for every need.

Lo ! other men have tracked thy woe,
　　From fountains of the heart,
The blessings or the blastings flow,
　　Which make thee as thou art.

BROTHERLY LOVE.

" Not for that we have dominion over your faith, but are helpers of your joy: for by faith ye stand."—2 Cor. i. 24.

" If there be any other commandment, it is briefly comprehended in this saying, namely, Thou shalt love thy neighbor as thyself."—Rom. xiii. 9.

" Let us not therefore judge one another any more; but judge this rather, that no man put a stumbling-block, or an occasion to fall, in his brother's way."—Rom. xiv. 13.

"Let every one of us please his neighbor for his good to edification."— Rom. xv. 2.

I T is doubtless a matter of the first import- *The resources of Religion.* ance to the Christian inquirer, that he should distinguish between the universality of the offers of Divine Grace which are extended from heaven for the salvation of our naturally benighted and wandering souls, and the extent of their efficacy for that great end, which can of course be universal only so far as their express conditions are complied with. While duly realizing this distinction, he will not, on the one hand, hastily and slothfully accept the creed of those who style themselves Universalists in religion, by rejecting that righteous fear which is "a fountain of life to depart from the snares of death;" nor will he, on the other, limit or undervalue the universality and magnitude of the mercy by which an earnest of the heavenly inheritance is revealed in the earthly experience of all, as a lure to our lost home, and, if accepted and followed in the cross to our corrupt nature, as a support and encouragement in the profitable work of truth and righteousness. Thus may we be prepared, without sacrificing the purity of our faith, to accept the doctrine that "God is the Saviour of all men," although "especially of those that believe;" (1 Tim. iv. 10) and that He has prepared gifts "for the rebellious also, that the Lord God might dwell amongst them." (Ps. lxviii. 18) The promises, that the wrath of man shall praise God, and that all things shall work together for the benefit of his faithful servants, are also thus rendered credible as to their possibility, and intelligible as to their fulfillment; since it appears that the error of the transgressor, so long at least as the treasury of grace may not be to him exhausted, consists not so much in a positive evil inherent in his outward act, as in the simple vice of will by which he prefers a meaner blessing to a greater one which is equally awaiting his acceptance. The works of such may thus evidently become undesigned testimonials to the glory of God, and means of wholesome discipline, if not of present consolation to their fellow-men, even while tending, by the willful blindness of the doers, to their own present or permanent loss. The dispensations of God in his outward providence, whether affecting us through the agency of the righteous man or of the sinner, are seen to be alike consonant with the inward manifestations of his grace, and to be, like them, though in varying degrees, co-ordinate influences in the Divine government of the world.

These preliminary suggestions upon the actual co-operation of an involuntary principle of beneficence in the human agents, with that which is voluntary, or benevolent as well as beneficent, in the relations and conduct of social life, will, I hope, secure the reader from being startled or confused by the presumed combination of them, which I have adopted as the basis of some practical observations on the duties of social intercourse.

The lesson of Death. It is recorded of the celebrated Sir James Mackintosh, that, on the eve of his departure from the world of time, his mind was remarkably clothed with awe, in contemplating the mysterious realities which he felt to be involved in his impending change. Quick to appreciate the threatening aspect of his physical condition, he seemed to regard it as opening a comparatively fresh field for the exertion of his naturally noble and well-practiced power of thought:

but the labor of intellect appeared to end only in perplexity, and he confessed, reverently and repeatedly, that there was much connected with the beneficent career of Christ which he could not understand. The decisive crisis which was soon to usher him, as in the twinkling of an eye, from the preparatory scenes and associations which he had so largely adorned and enjoyed, into the realms of unfading glory and unfettered fellowship upon which he was doubtless about to enter, seemed to him as a deep, if not a dreadful, gulf, as it must seem to all who do not fully realize the power of religious faith to emancipate the soul from the bondage of our natural state, in all its circumstances and consequences. It would seem that he had not thus learned the apostolic doctrine, that the just man must live at all times by this very faith, so that the appointed means of salvation, being yet unrecognized or not duly appreciated, could not close up the fearful abyss in which our sins and infirmities must otherwise naturally terminate, as tributary channels leading to an ocean of darkness. Intellect was baffled, but the Light of Grace triumphed. The resources of worldly prudence, and the fruits of mere morality or conventional culture, availed him not; but the work of the Mediator, as immediately revealed from heaven, and realized in his own heart through the obedience of faith, banished every doubt. To one who said, "Jesus Christ loves you," his reply was, "Jesus Christ— Love—the same thing!" Afterward, on his simply saying, "I believe," and his attendant inquiringly adding, "In God?" he replied, "In Jesus."

Sir James Mackintosh may be said to have been, especially and pre-eminently, a moralist. His professional labors, his literary pursuits, and his extended intercourse with general society, testified in many ways that he was an almost lifelong student of Law, in the broadest meaning of that term : and such a life, and such a death, together considered, may be offered as a remarkable confirmation of the apostolic testimony that "love is the fulfilling of the law."

2

Essential compre-hensiveness of Divine Love.   The Divine Love, it must be confessed, is the largest and highest theme which can occupy the thoughts of man. Flowing immediately from the Creative Cause of every derivative good, it is both the vitalizing power and the crowning fruit of all true knowledge. It is thus in itself both the worthy object of Christian aspiration, and also the means by which the humbly believing and simply self-denying seeker attains to a participation in the sublime mysteries and pure pleasures of eternal truth and spiritual life. It is self-fulfilling and self-preserving, rescuing from the wreck of our fallen nature the divided and scattered, and still struggling, members of the first Adam, and binding them, by the inspiration of the second Adam, into its own "bundle of life." Here they find that renewed self-hood, in which personal individuality, through the sacrifice of the will, becomes compatible with that true fellowship, whose roots are within them, and lie deeper than the facts and forms of nature. The very ground of emulation and contention is renounced, and they become the adopted children of God, and brethren and joint heirs with Christ.

Practical limitation of its efficacy, the ground of subsidiary Law.   Love is thus the fulfilling of the law, because it is the fulfilling of itself. As it is, indeed, an inseparable attribute of the Omnipotent and Omnipresent Deity, the question may seem naturally to arise, Why need any labor to experience it, or offer to expound it, since it must be able and willing to manifest itself? Omnipotence is truly an awful theme, and one which must ever be unapproachable by man, in its ground or essence, as distinguished from its manifestations. Law, however, or Fate, as distinguished from freedom, is a subject which especially demands the attention of imperfect beings who are capable of struggling against their imperfections, inasmuch as it may possibly be opened to their inquiry by the very fact of its having some origin apart from the perfect will of Omnipo-

tence. The curse of those who "came not to the help of the
Lord, to the help of the Lord against the mighty" (Judges, v.
23), is but one of the scriptural evidences that even the power
of Omnipotence may not be, in every sense of the term, all-
comprehensive. It is enough for us to know decisively, that it
will be all-sufficient for our present and everlasting welfare, upon
our acceptance of the terms prescribed for that effect. Its power
will then indeed be "Omnipotence," so far as our experience
can extend, and an Omnipotence which may be all the more
adequately realized by us, the more necessary our co-operation
may have been for its manifestation in us. But that there may
nevertheless be some other power, outside of any omnipotence
which we can assume to exist, which can, through our own consent, influence us as free agents to refuse good and choose evil,
is rendered sufficiently possible to our apprehension by the
simple analogy of mathematical science ; in which we find that
there may be supposed various infinite or incomprehensible
quantities, which, by the mere circumstance of their being infinite, must be practically equal in our finite calculations, and
which yet in themselves shall be most unequal. Reason, therefore, no more than experience, can clash with the vague testimony of recorded revelation and the crude sentiment of bygone
ages, that there is a spiritual or indestructible Power of evil, which
is infinite in itself, and yet essentially alien and inferior to the
God of Love. By farther simply surmising this Evil Power to
be self-existent, or co-eternal with the High and Holy One, who
is the Author of the creation and the supreme Controller of the
material universe, and thus capable of attracting to itself the
wayward will of the immortal principle in man, we are enabled
to assign a conceivable origin and a beneficent operation to all
the fetters of Law, consistently with that element of necessity
through which it is experimentally known to us all, as either our
ruler or our servant. We may deplore the mixture of evil
while accepting the whole truth as we find it filling our several
measures of experience ; but if we sincerely prize our privileges
as beings who are capable of looking beyond the limitations of

the present,* we will not turn away from the imperfect promise of hope which is offered to us in the temporary bondage of Law.   The law written upon stone has long been abrogated in favor of the progressive law which is written "upon the fleshy tables of the heart," and which now summons the world onward to perfection ; but this also may be regarded as being, in its turn, but a law of principles, which are to be honored by being successively abandoned for others which are more comprehensive, until that perfect Life of Love is revealed, in the prevalence of which the dispensation of the Gospel is being continually inaugurated, and shall finally be fully established. So far, therefore, as this Divine Life may fall short of entire prevalence, the necessity must remain for a law which may be investigated and expounded, as the clearest attainable manifestation of Love, and for the exercise of that authority in which the earnest believer shall say to his halting brother, " Know the Lord."   It is in the profound realization of my own infirmity

---

* " My creed," wrote the late Henry Colman, " resolves itself into a very simple proposition—God is wise and good.   He is as wise and good as wise and good can be, and under his government and providence I feel a perfect security.   Whatever appearances may present themselves to my limited and imperfect observation, I have no doubt that the final result will be all that the best mind could desire. . . . . I cannot look upon the human being with all the beautiful endowments of mind which pertain to him, and all the high moral attributes which so elevate his nature, and all the charming affections, sentiments, and hopes, which seem to stamp him as divine; I cannot look upon such a being advancing continually in intellectual and moral attainments, rising by self-discipline above everything sensual and worldly, and in the elevation and expansion of his views and purposes breathing a far purer atmosphere than this low world affords; I cannot, I say, look upon such a being as destined only for a region of existence where his advances are continually restricted, and where soon his progress must be arrested, and all his attainments, noble as they may be, must come to naught, and be scattered like the gilded and burnished clouds which are scarcely seen, and their outlines hardly defined, before the wind sweeps them away for ever."   It would perhaps be hard to find in so small a compass a more eloquent or a much more accurate assertion of the triumph of freedom over necessity, through the intervention of law or discipline.

that I thus venture to give utterance, as briefly as I may, to some suggestions for the consideration of any who may find them suggestive, upon the subject or law of Brotherly Love.

So large a part of our life consists of our social duties and privileges—our social affections and aspirations indeed hold so predominating and engrossing a place even among our natural wants as rational beings—that we may safely speak of the spontaneous love or regard, which the great mass of mankind experience for those of their fellows with whom they can mingle and sympathize on the before mentioned ground of natural congeniality and providential beneficence, as the actual law of their life. As all human conduct is liable to the seductions of a lawless caprice, this natural love, being a leading and comparatively permanent influence, cannot lose its real rank as a law from the circumstance that its operation may be obscured by the confused workings of a many-membered and short-sighted selfishness. It may indeed be said to originate in selfishness, in so far as it must originally impress our fallen nature through the force of selfish considerations. It accordingly derives all its stability and validity, such as they are, from the fact that there is always, in any community, a characteristic average of enlightenment as to the means of pleasure or happiness ; and its operation will be obscured or confused, not so much by any deficiency which may exist, or by any deterioration which may occur in this average standard of action, as by the greater or less variety and discrepancy of the individual qualifications and dispositions which may be thereby represented as the general character of the community. It will be chiefly as our law itself is upon this ground, more or less definite, that its operation will be more or less uniform.

Brotherly Love the motive and sanction of Law.

The great evidence of a Providential agency in the government of the world lies in the fact that the characters of men, whether singly or in the mass, are found to be adapted to

Traceable even in the suggestions of fear, as Divine Love is in the revelations of fact.

2 *   I:

their external circumstances, with which again their duties and
their interests flow in close and parallel connection, like the so-
called "induced currents" of electrical action,—their duties
corresponding with their characters, as their interests do with
their circumstances. Owing to the assimilating influence of
established institutions, consequent upon the comparative stability of enlightened institutions, the power of the social law thus
determined by the character of a community, is most apparent
in civilized or cultivated life; but is probably discoverable in
every condition of society, through the veil of conflicting but
self-limited violations and apparent exceptions, and may safely
be styled a natural "Law of Love," although it cannot be said
to imply the elevated brotherly love which flows from conscious
communion with the common Father, who is the inexhaustible
Source of love, but may, on the contrary, often degenerate,
through an unworthy choice of the objects of love, into a Law
of Fear.

Perfect attainability
and efficacy of Broth-
erly Love as an ele-
ment of the Christian
dispensation.

Inasmuch, however, as all love for our fellow-beings as intelligent creatures, is, in a natural and obvious sense of the word, brotherly,
and may even be regarded in every case as
one of the gifts of present happiness which
were purchased for man by the propitiatory sacrifice of our
adorable Saviour; inasmuch, also, as the very communion of
the saints, which is more worthily styled "Brotherly Love,"
when weakly regarded or condescendingly acknowledged as an
object desirable in itself, or as a mere means for any finite or
worldly end, must, if not wholly lost in such dangerous eagerness or connivance, partake of the imperfection which characterizes every attainment when known out of its subordination to
the ever present and all-sustaining Giver; it would seem that
the phrase "Brotherly Love" may be fairly adopted as practically synonymous with the natural "Law of Love" before
spoken of, and as representing a working means or influence
which is universally at hand, and strictly congenial to the

natural imperfections of mankind in their probational estate, and which still serves as "a school-master" to bring souls unto Christ.

In either view of its development, there- Its pretensions as a
fore, it appears that Love, so far as it may be law of duty invite
embodied or exemplified in the facts and cir- scrutiny.
cumstances of social intercourse, brings along with it an intelligible law, and becomes indeed the very fountain of law. So far, therefore, as there is occasion for recognizing law in anything, there is occasion for recognizing a Law of Brotherly Love. In other words, Love, so far as it may ever be an intelligible and practical principle, is by no means an irresponsible principle; but its pretensions must always be open to question in the Spirit of Love, both as to its means and as to its objects. This doctrine may perhaps appear to the reader to be too evident in itself to require such a detailed demonstration; but it is fundamentally important that its truth should be deeply appreciated, in order that the profession of love may not become a rule of darkness rather than of light, as it is in danger of becoming where the willful ambiguity and reserve are indulged in, by which love may be confounded with dissimulation.

There is therefore a Law or Rule of Love Test-principle, the
by which all men who claim the sympathy of reasonable hope of
their fellow-beings are responsible to one an- conferring pleasure.
other. (This law, in its simplest and most obvious expression, is nothing more or less than the suppression of selfishness in thought, word and deed, in our dealings with one another. It is the ceasing "to do evil," in order that we may "learn to do well." In other words, it is the abandoning, so far as possible, of our own transient interests and fallible opinions, in deference to those of our neighbors, and in the faith that all interests and all opinions must be alike temporary and illusory, which cannot be recognized as realities from whatever direction they are candidly contemplated. \It rarely indeed, if ever, occurs, that men are driven by their mere physical necessities

to the point of actual conflict, or are forced to maintain their dissimilar opinions in the form of dogmatic assertion or of direct contradiction. The encroachments of violence in either mode may be traced to the deficiency, rather than to the excess, of that sure power which attends an insight into the opulence of nature and the universality of truth. The Law of Love thus has room for free play, both in the prevention of open selfishness and in the mortification of secret conceit. To this effect we may interpret the testimony of the careful observer and thinker already mentioned and quoted, as it occurs in his diary at a date of twenty years previous to his decease. "A benevolent man," says he, "estimates others by the degree in which he can make them happy ; a selfish man, by the degree in which he can make them subservient to his own interest. To estimate human beings merely or chiefly by their intrinsic merits, and to act towards them on that principle, is a proud pretension, but evidently inconsistent with the condition of human nature. It would be natural in mere spectators, but not in those who are themselves engaged in the race of life. The evident effect of it is, after all, to cheat ourselves. When we suppose that we are estimating others on principles of severe justice, we may be giving judgment on them under the influence of dislike, disgust, or anger." With the exception that the writer seems to ascribe our fallibility rather to the limitation of our circumstances than to the feebleness of our vision, the wisdom embodied in these remarks is perhaps as intrinsically pure as it is practically important. It may be observed that we are not even told that the benevolent man will estimate others by the degree in which he may think he can make them better than they are. This would evidently involve the judgment which the writer deprecates, and which the Gospel of Love never enjoins, as to the spiritual condition, in the sight of God, of those with whom we have to do. Doubtless, few knew better than Sir James how difficult it is at all times, and especially in extreme or sudden cases, to avoid impressions and to lay aside prepossessions as to the secrets of individual character ; but he doubtless also understood that such conceptions are most likely to be useful, if not also to be truthful, where they are the spontaneous growth of a heart which is animated by the light of love, and so influenced by them unconsciously rather than presumptuously. At the same time probably no one would more readily have admitted, that the way to make men happy is not willfully to abet or countenance them in the pursuit of criminal or vicious courses. Probably he would have considered it the part of charity to take it for granted that they are desirous to avoid or escape from such courses, or that they at least will be (as few indeed will not) when their senses are fully aroused to see their disastrous tendency, and therefore to prepare them for such a view as gently, and as quickly, and even as candidly, as possible. Thus, we may presume, he would have been able to sympathize with that stirring strain of a celebrated investigator and teacher* of our own country and our own age:

> " Love's hearts are faithful, but not fond;
> Bound for the just, but not beyond :
> Not glad, as the low-loving herd,
> Of self in other still preferred ;
> But they have heartily designed
> The benefit of broad mankind.
> And they serve men austerely,
> After their own genius, clearly,
> Without a false humility.
> For this is Love's nobility—
> Not to scatter bread and gold,
> Goods and raiment bought and sold ;
> But to hold fast his simple sense,
> And speak the speech of innocence,
> And with hand, and body, and blood,
> To make his bosom-counsel good.
> For he that feeds men serveth few ;
> He serves all who dares be true."

Administration.   External conflict and discord are ever the result and the measure of internal confusion.
* R. W. EMERSON.

The Christian warfare is that in which the true believer struggles
to observe and to obey that Light of Life revealed in his own
soul, by which, as it is suffered to have free course, all the fruits
of darkness are exposed.   As this result is realized, the delusions of selfishness will be scattered and banished, and he will
experience a humbling but cheering sense of surprise, on finding
how truly superficial and impotent to annoy is every external
occasion of offence, whether it consist in the mere limitation
of physical necessity, or in the random trespass of the passing
stranger, or in the systematic siege of the household foe, save
as it may be naturally more or less competent to enlist and in-
cite the lusts of his own heart which war in his own members.
Surprise itself will vanish in its turn, as he proceeds to observe
that selfishness, wherever existing, is so contracted in its very
nature, that its seemingly most aggressive and most malicious
outburst can be nothing more than a manifestation of spiritual
slothfulness through its readiest mode of expression.   Dis-
covering that no natural disposition or appetite can find vent
in a debasing gratification, except by the weak or rash sacrifice
of an ennobling alternative, and having learned that the human
will is never truly acting save when it is directing nature rather
than acquiescing with it, he may adopt, in a sense perhaps
deeper and broader than that in which it was uttered, the dec-
laration of the excellent Hannah More, that "Idleness, though
itself the most unperforming of all the vices, is the pass
through which they all enter, the stage upon which they all act."

Consummation.   I will conclude this rambling labor of ci-
tation and comment, by briefly remarking upon
another fragment of the dying testimony of the British moralist
and statesman, as to the value of the "royal law"* of Brotherly
Love.   "There is nothing," said he, "*so* right in the world as
to cultivate and exercise kindness—the most certainly evan-
gelical of all doctrines—*the* principle of Jesus Christ."   We
should doubless deceive ourselves by assigning, as these words

* JAM. ii. 8.

might be construed to assign, to this second commandment of the Christian dispensation, an importance superior to that of the first. But when we remember that we are told by our Divine Teacher that the second is like unto the first, we may at least infer that the due appreciation of either will involve that of the other. May we cherish them together in our hearts, and preach them together in our lives !

THE PACIFIC CABLE.

As brothers part at morn,
　To join at even
With day-long labor worn,
　And count it heaven;

So Adam's family,
　Sped far asunder,
Shall meet in amity,
　With worship-wonder.

Some, turning from the sun,
　The earth have rambled,
And all its treasures won,
　Or for them scrambled.

Some, watchful of the skies,*
　Pursued the morning,
Thirsting with eager eyes
　For its adorning.

And still our early traits
　Appear to linger,
And point from present straits
　With prophet-finger.

May we, in self-defence
　From doom of Edom,
Mix Eastern reverence
　With Western freedom!

That each to each may say,
　Have done with sorrow!
The world hath had its day;
　Give God the morrow!

6th Mo. 1860.

* The red disk in the national ensign of Japan has been supposed to represent the rising
sun.

22

THE CHRISTIAN PENAL SYSTEM.

"Say not thou, I will recompense evil: but wait on the Lord and he shall save thee." PROV. xx. 22.

"Michael the Archangel, when contending with the Devil he disputed about the body of Moses, durst not bring against him a railing accusation, but said, The Lord rebuke thee." JUDE, 9.

THE practical mysteries which are involved in the abstract doctrines of the Divine Omniscience, Omnipresence and potential Supremacy, are unfathomable only in so far as they are inexhaustible. The Faith of to-day cannot live upon the manna of yesterday ; but materials can never be wanting for its subsistence while the occasion for its exercise shall remain ; and the essential work of the Christian, it should be ever remembered, is indistinguishable from his essential meat, whether it be called the "Work of Faith" or the "Labor of Love." If there be any universally instantaneous stage in the experience of Christian conversion, such presumably is the extinction of the blindness of Faith in the vision of Love. The subordinate objects, modes and fruits of Faith continually multiply in the path of the Christian, until Faith and Hope become finally alike obsolete in the immediate realization of that one Truth, Way and Life, from which all partial manifestations of good proceed, to which they are designed to lead, and in which they are capable of being harmoniously blended.

Of these subordinate truths or objects of Faith, there are two of which it is especially important for the sake of social order that they should be recognized as indisputable realities.

3

One of these is the promise abundantly held forth in Holy
Writ, that "bread shall be given and waters shall be sure,"
that the means of living and doing shall not be wanting, to
the servants of God.   The other is the duty and privilege revealed in the New Testament, of believing "all things" in
the exercise of gospel-charity.   Except the human judge be
gifted on any occasion with the divine prerogative of an infallible discernment to the contrary, it is always possible for
him to believe, and therefore always incumbent on him to
assume, that his fellow-beings are endeavoring to do rightly
so far as they may be free agents.   The extent to which they
are indeed free agents, is of course known only to Him who
is conversant with all their past history and with all their
present merely circumstantial limitations, and who knows
how far they may still continue to be in any respects the
slaves of habit and the pamperers of passion, without shut-
ting "the gates of mercy" on their own souls.   The first of
these objects or rules of Faith may be styled the principle of
social independence, and is here noticeable as the logical
foundation of the second, which may be designated as the
principle of social influence.

Little reflection is necessary to understand that the transgressor who is treated as one who is doing his very best, must
be treated most severely and most efficiently.   And the more
angry he may become at having it assumed, in the absence of
his own open self-condemnation, that he could not do better,
the more glaringly will he justify the disciplinary measures
of those who may have proceeded to act on the assumption.
Almost as obvious is the remark that the merely formal well-
doer is always the most easily kept within the reach of wholesome influence, by being treated as a well-meaner.   For even
hypocrisy cannot at last avoid drawing the contrast between
itself and earnestness, and so being reformed, if anything can
reform it, by the sense of its own surpassing shame.   The
precept and the promise, "Vengeance is mine; I will repay,
saith the Lord," like all the other mysteries of Faith, become

ever increasingly fathomable with the increase of knowledge and the development of mind, and increasingly illustrative of the general principle. "the just shall live by his faith," and of the corresponding general injunction, " Trust to the Lord with thy whole heart, and lean not to thine own understanding."

INFLUENCE.

A MAUDLIN mood by cunning caught;
   A current, turned from nature's course,
   On private aims to spend its force
By subtle machinations taught;

A flood, unstable as the will
   Which rests upon a borrowed faith;
   A lawless league; a reckless wraith
At random prone to cure or kill;

So facile, and so purposeless,
   Seems oft the strength which all men know
   Through others on themselves to flow,
In violence or gentleness.

From crooked paths the way direct
   Appears to bend.   So doth the heart
   Not moored by hope, seem to impart
To things around, its own defect.

In rigid course the truth still flows:
   E'en language when it thus affirms
   Some lameness shows, in that it terms
The truth, a thing which comes and goes:

But stabler than the electric ground
   Which underlies all matter; o'er
   The gulf of outward distance, more
Alert to waft the secret sound

Of deep exclaiming unto deep;
   Doth truth to hearts attentive prove
   Its work, and only seem to move
In darkness, to the souls which sleep.

OUR CHAOS.

"God is light."—1 JOHN i. 5.
"God is not the author of confusion, but of peace."—1 COR. xiv. 33.

HAD our blessed Saviour, on the occasion of his appearance as a man among men, commanded his disciples to "be perfect" as He was perfect, the precept might have been ever after adduced as evidence that example, rather than independent enlightenment and decision,—that precedent rather than principle,—was the divinely authorized means of governing the world. By directing their attention on the other hand to an invisible and ever-progressive standard,—our conception of the infinite purity and power of the Heavenly Father,—he enforced the necessity of individual investigation, and established the doctrine of individual responsibility. It is impossible for the unregenerate human mind to divest itself of the impression that power in some way resides, and is therefore to be sought for, in creaturely attainment, rather than in a spiritual and essentially progressive union with the divine Creator. We wander at best in an inveterate and deceitful confusion of truth and beauty, until the supernatural power of faith in Christ shall subordinate the earthward to the heavenward nature, and lift us out of the inherited limitations which prevent us from recognizing the essential unity of the diverse aspects of truth. We must, more or less, have chaos in ourselves, and discordance with one another, until we learn on this inward ground of coherency and assurance, to distinguish between cause and effect in every definite portion of our experience.

3 *

The rule of Theology here becomes the rule of all science and the test of all art. As there is no safe beginning, so there is no worthy ending, but in God; and every assumption, and every aim which deliberately falls short of acknowledging his omnipresent power and goodness, is self-refuted and self-defeated, in the view of any who have become acquainted with the Source and course of true inspiration. The manna of the wilderness which lasted but for a day, is an enduring type of practical wisdom, so long as that wilderness journey itself remains an unfulfilled type. The perishable creatures can only be truly estimated and safely pursued in their graduated and ever-varying subordination to the eternal Creator, and to one another in Him. What this subordination at any particular juncture may be, mortals cannot of course be expected to decide for one another, since the leadership of mind is itself a variable phenomenon, imperfectly symbolized in any natural or artificial distinctions, save as the lines of distinction in science and in society shall be viewed from that Centre of divine illumination and life—that "fullness of God,"*—in which they meet and terminate. It is enough for all practically to remember that subordination, mediate or immediate, and not self-preservation, is "the first law" of the better nature, wherein obedience becomes the sole condition of endless life and perfect order. "Let us hear the conclusion of the whole matter: Fear God, and keep his commandments, for this is the whole duty of man."†

* Eph. iii. 19.   † Eccles. xii. 13.

FORTUNE.

"How rudely broken into bits
    Is this promiscuous whole !
How miserably sometimes fits
    Its circumstance, the soul !

"This mess we call society,
    As known in outward things—
What ruinous variety
    Its boasted order brings !

"The soul's the substance of the man :
    Are not all souls alike ?
Then how unfair the social plan,
    In which such contrasts strike !

"My neighbor has the very lot
    Which would be bliss to me,
With grief or pother scarce a jot,
    So far as I can see.

"Surely, some savage solitude
    Were fitter to my mind,
Where such hard thoughts could not intrude,
    Nor envy of my kind !"

Not so, most wayward !   Thou canst own
    The soul to be the man ;
But yet the wrongs thou wouldst bemoan,
    Thou wilt not stay to scan.

Thy neighbor knows his private grief :
    And thou, if thou wilt see,
May'st find the pleasures of his fief
    An heritage to thee.

THE RULE OF POVERTY.

I CANNOT doubt that the famous founder of the Order of the Franciscans was and is a genuine saint. I do not venture to decide on the truth or falsity of the story of his having received in hands and feet and side, the *stigmata* of his crucified Lord; and I consider that it would be equally rash to recommend his vow of perpetual poverty to all conditions of men in all ages of the world. His memory is illustrious with me, mainly by virtue of his plain-spoken precept, "Let every man remember that such as he may appear in the sight of God, such he really is." I fancy that I observe in this utterance a combination of filial dependence and manly independence, which show it glaringly in contrast with that too popular strain of an erratic modern minstrel,

> "O wad some power the giftie gie us
> To see oursels as ithers see us!"

I consider that if we are but careful not to shun poverty, it is unnecessary and inexpedient, as a general rule, to go to the length of actually seeking it. Says a contemporary,*

> 'Twas not wisely done,
> On all to bind that ecstasy of love
> Which revels in privations. Well for him,
> The stainless-hearted knight of poverty,
> That wandering through the world, as one who lacks
> His daily bread. But, for the feebler souls,
> The beggar's life may bring the beggar's thoughts,

* Prof. PLUMPTRE, *Master and Scholar.*

The sordid care, the coarse and earthly greed,
The baser that all gloss and finer touch
Are torn away, and nothing left to hide
The swine-like foulness."

The advantage of every condition of life may be said to consist solely in its adaptedness to the character of the liver. In other words, the happiness and usefulness of all men depend, under the guidance of heavenly grace, only on that correspondence between their several characters and circumstances, which is the continual proof of a Providential control in human affairs, and without which the great practical doctrine of divine contentment and devout thankfulness through all the vicissitudes of life, apart from the hope of a still more blissful hereafter, would be a manifest heresy. To the faithful Christian, life itself is such absolute and unfathomable wealth, that all the degrees of material and intellectual attainment, and of merely imitative culture, by which men are distinguished when compared among themselves, are indeed but " as the small dust of the balance" in his estimation. Where there is but that fitness on the part of any to their several surroundings, of which the prevalence of thankful contentment is the indisputable proof, there must be lessons of universal interest to be derived from such surroundings, even if they be remarkable only as those of comparative destitution.

The advantage of the condition of poverty lies, doubtless, in the fact that it is pre-eminently a condition of discipline. In a world where discipline may be said to be the only universally important object of life, as being the only means for realizing the riches of a nobler world, this circumstance might indeed seem to recommend the vow of the Franciscans, were it not that the purely spiritual discipline of the Cross of Christ is of itself sufficient under all circumstances, to lead him who is the subject of it to the realization of the heavenly life. The peculiar advantage of contented poverty, therefore, must lie in the peculiar facilities which it may afford for the apprehension and extension of that truly and only divine discipline.

C

"The world, the flesh and the devil," are the great foes
which in all ages beset the mind, the body and the soul, of
the Christian pilgrim.   The use of poverty as a guard against
the dangers of fleshly indulgence, I deem too obvious for comment.   Its utility as a weapon for contending with the great
"adversary of souls," where the appetites and the thoughts
are rightly ordered, we may well doubt, inasmuch as all sorts
of attainment here become available for the vindication of
truth.   It therefore only remains to consider how a cheerful
acquiescence in this condition of life may assist in overcoming
the Evil One, when we meet with him neither as an open
tempter in the house of feasting, nor as an open accuser in
the house of mourning, but rather as a companion in the
highway of social life, elaborately disguised with all the superficial graces of "the prince of the power of the air, the
spirit that now worketh in the children of disobedience."

The aid which a superficially apparent poverty here brings
to the Christian soldier, consists in the simple fact, that it
furnishes him with a mask which is still more effectual than
that with which he has to contend.   The apparent felicity of
"the children of disobedience," if at all deceptive to him, is
less so than his apparent misery is to them.   His circumstances ensure to him that ready contempt which removes the
only disguise of their character, the only objects of their ambition or double-mindedness being there comparatively wanting, and therefore practically absent.   Affectation being with
them the language of respect, it is only in the company of
those whom they despise, that they can make any approach
to sincerity.   Thus it happens that the canine nature which
fawns and cringes before the insignia of worldly power, cannot conceal its lupine lineage from the eye and ear of those
who have discovered, either in their own experience or in
that of others, the real resources of poverty.

No artificial system of espionage can approach in efficiency
to that which is thus Providentially maintained in the career
of those, who "using the world as not abusing it," are the

true rulers of the world, to the extent of the talents severally committed to them. " Notwithstanding," let such heed the warning of the Divine Leader and Teacher, " in this rejoice not, that the spirits are subject unto you, but rather rejoice because your names are written in heaven."

A L'EMPEREUR.

ABAFT, like pilot at his helm,
    As truth obscure,
The simple freeman guides his mystic realm
    A l'empereur.

He dimly sees the difference
    More known than seen,
Between the show and substance of events
    In life terrene :

Yet well he knows how faint his sight ;
    And farther knows,
That, as the world revolves through day and night,
    Its harvest grows.

So cares he not to stoop his eyes
    To watch the growth,
But sows and reaps in season, as the skies
    Direct for both.

Whate'er the field, he cares to know
    Force, more than form,
Braced, whether zephyrs or tornados blow,
    To stem the storm.

He views, unblinded by desires
    For vain eclât,
How every falling crisis still requires
    Its *coup d'etat ;*

And as each Rubicon is passed
    With purpose pure,
Good angels call to the serene outcast,*
    —*Vive l'empereur !*

34
        * 1 Cor. iv. 13.

HOME-LIFE.

"Let love be without dissimulation." ROM. xii. 9.

IT is well said that "Charity begins at home." Only in
the corrupt creeds and codes which tend in some way to
enslave man to his fellow-mortal, can the contrary doctrine
gain place. Peace and war alike originate in the heart. As
the sure policy of mercy does not lessen its excellence, so the
seeming impunity of tyranny does not qualify its disgraceful-
ness. The despot, of whatever sort or degree, is but a disguised and successful beggar, who lives upon the forbearance
or the ignorance of his victims. The corner-stone of his imposture lies in the artful insinuation that the first duty of a
subject is to an earthly ruler or to a prevailing fashion, rather
than to himself and to his God. The true subordination of
both Church and State is thus more or less subverted; the
very family is divided against itself, and the barriers of prejudice, which conceal the possible freedom of divine grace
from the actual slavery of human nature, to the same degree
confirmed. Individual independence is the necessary basis of
social subordination, harmony and intelligence. Enlightened
self-interest, although by no means a guaranty of the enlightened self-sacrifice which is the soul of the Christian life,
is the only principle of nature which that spiritual motive can
immediately and effectually address. The ecclesiastical, or
political, or social propagandist, who advocates any other ma-
ternity for the individual idea of duty, is essentially a beggar
or a brigand, who sows selfishness instead of charity, and can
reap only disappointment. Surely it is well that both rulers

4   35

and subjects should cherish the doctrine, that a man's life, be
it the life of charity or that of selfishness, cannot begin elsewhere than at home!

The battle of life must be fought at home. The senti-
mentalist who maintains that successful life is a mere development of nature under any definable course of culture,
must indeed assume the state of peace to be an heir-loom of
nature; but he must find himself at length at fault, both in
the individual and in the social application of his doctrine.
The indefinable law of the spiritual cross is the only rule
which can enforce that continual subjection of the natural
will which is comparable to the death of the germinant seed
in the covering soil. All preconceived notions of happiness
and harmony must be subordinated, if not sacrificed, to the
continual revelation of the inexhaustible Spirit of Good, or
happiness and harmony will be empty names. Premeditation, or dependence upon preconception, implies a subjection
to the limitations of time; whereas eternity is the element of
the soul, whose only healthy and lasting dependence must be
upon the Divine Word, which "is not bound" by any of the
limitations of time, space, or language. If the show of order
remains where the will of the one omnipresent and divine
Ruler is not freely acknowledged as the accessible and ultimate standard of duty, it can only be because beggarly Fear
has proportionally usurped the throne of beneficent Love.
The principle of fear cannot indeed be dispensed with, so
long as the bondage of sin shall in any degree survive in
individuals or in the world; but the triumph of life consists
in its voluntary subjugation to the mystical but omnipotent
dominion of Charity.

The triumph of life must be found at home. Glorious
indeed is the triumph of the life of charity; for the whole
world—yes, the whole universe, is its home. Its expansive
virtue demands infinitude for its development. If it indeed
begin at home, its genuineness will be incontrovertible, and
its prowess irresistible. Conquests and coalitions will crowd

upon its career, and crowns of rejoicing will everywhere reward the soldiers of faith. Confusion, on the other hand, and bankruptcy beyond the hope even of beggary, will be the inevitable doom of the faithless soldiers of fortune, who shall have incapacitated themselves, by the eagerness of selfishness, from enjoying the overflowing pleasures of the divine life. " How shall we escape if we neglect so great salvation ?"

NATURE.

As culture is not intuition ;
  As knowledge is not merit ;
As lust bespeaks a base ambition,
  And will, a ruling spirit ;

If faith be not a galling fetter,
  Nor hope a weak illusion,
Nor love a loose and lifeless letter,
  Nor truth a grand confusion ;

Man's life affords an aspect double,
  An upper and an under,
Which fools may try with barren trouble
  To simplify or sunder.

For nature waits a trusty servant
  As on a faithful master,
While'er the soul abides observant
  Of profit and disaster :

While, true to its allotted station,
  By sure experience lighted,*
It works the wonderful salvation
  In which all wrongs are righted.

Then nature finds her beauty youthful,
  With more than culture polished ;
While knowledge is as strong as truthful,
  And slavish lust abolished :

She shines with a divine reflection
  In all her turns and features,
A mirror lent for self-detection
  To self-deluded creatures.

* PHIL. iii. 16.

THE REIGN OF PEACE.

" Set thine house in order, for thou shalt die and not live."—2 KINGS xx.

THE origin of order, like that of every blessing and of every curse, of all life and of all action, is in the realm of spiritual experience. It may indeed be seriously questioned, as it certainly has been doubted by intelligent observers. whether there can be any actual consciousness in any other than spiritual beings ; and without consciousness there can obviously be no such thing as experience. The freedom of heaven and the bondage of hell, sometimes incidentally confused, but always essentially distinct from each other, may be said to be the animating principles of human experience ; and however they may be temporarily veiled from our apprehension by our necessary intercourse with the things of space and time, they will be finally revealed to us, either to our joy or to our sorrow, as the inward substance of the outward manifestations in which they are at once incorporated and obscured to our natural perceptions. Order, or simplicity in multiplicity, is the language of truth to the truly attentive ear. The very unity of the Deity, so far as it is capable of intellectual demonstration, is but the logical consequence of the universal simplicity of truth. Truth, by being essentially a simple thing, is a book ever open and legible to the true lovers of order ; and hence, if we believe the power of light to be indeed superior to that of darkness, we must infer that order is the first law, not merely of the spiritual, but also of the natural, world. It is the principle through which the presence of the Almighty and All-gracious Creator is reveal-

ed in his works to all who watch and strive against the entrance of confusion in those deep abodes of feeling which are
among the secret sources of thought.

Like any other partial and merely auxiliary blessing, indeed, order is not a thing which is to be found by seeking it
as an end. Since it is idolatry to pursue any good short of
the absolute and unfathomable will of our Heavenly Father
and Ruler exclusively for its own sake, we cannot be actually
dependent upon even the highest form of law while we are
the privileged subjects of free grace. The fear of the Lord
which is " the beginning of wisdom," is indeed the life of the
Law, until the perfect love which " casts out fear" becomes
the established bond of union between God and man, in the
new dispensation of perfect salvation. Truth, however, is a
thing which may be lawfully pursued and wisely loved for
its own sake, since it is the nature of .it to purge itself of all
blemishes which our blindness may impute to its appearance,
and to heal all the miseries which our diseased nature may
suffer from its operation, as it is indeed singly prized and
sought for. It is the divine principle in all the dispensations
of providence and of grace, and finally becomes to its faithful
followers but another name for the Deity as revealed in the
blessed and only Mediator between God and man. There
can thus be no genuine and effectual love of order which
may not be more worthily styled a pure love of Truth. The
warning therefore which was addressed to the prosperous
king of Judah, is applicable in all ages to all men in whom
the great work of life has not been perfected by their acceptance of the Divine Redeemer's universal offers upon his own
unvarying terms.

The question, then, forcibly presents itself, What is this
stronghold of order which we call Truth, and how is it to be
known? Truth may be said to be in itself the material or
substance of all healthy experience : in its relations to human
consciousness and conduct it may be styled the object of
faith and the fruit of consistency. " He that cometh to God

must believe that He is, and that He is a rewarder of them that diligently seek Him." The true earnestness of purpose in which past, present and future, are regarded but as different manifestations of eternity, and which accordingly values in all of them only those things which are of substantial and eternal interest, is the only spiritual qualification in any way originating in the exercise of our own free will, through which we can recognize the essential unity of Truth. As we thus become consistent in ourselves, we are enabled to appreciate the consistency which prevails among the seemingly heterogeneous objects of our knowledge, — a consistency which the sincere seeker ever finds to keep pace with the actual progress of his knowledge, and to be limited only by the barriers of his conscious ignorance. There is indeed an unconscious ignorance, or a blind conceitedness, which is ever ready to impute its own inconsistencies to the works of the All-wise Creator ; but they who are the subjects of it must at best be classed with the idle hearers of the word, ·whom the Apostle likened " to a man beholding his natural face in a glass, who goeth away and straightway forgetteth what manner of man he was." True faith may be said to be a spiritual travail, which results in the production of a communicable knowledge, and of visible works, which alike bear the family features of a divine system, however variously times and circumstances may limit or extend the capacities of individuals for such production. Truth will be not less to any the object of their faith and the fruit of their consistency, from the fact that the outward limitation of unusually imperfect· opportunities may disqualify them from becoming teachers to others, otherwise than as examples of the manifest felicity which rewards true earnestness. To such, no less than to the most accomplished expounders of nature and of doctrine, may be applied the remarkable testimony of a celebrated cotemporary. " Your true encyclopedical," says Thomas Carlyle in his essay on Diderot, " is the Homer, the Shakspeare ; every genuine poet is a living, embodied, real encyclopedia—in more or fewer volumes. Were his experience, his insight of details, never so limited, the whole world lies imaged as a whole within him." On the other hand, he continues:—"Whosoever has not seized the whole, cannot yet speak truly of any part, but will perpetually need new guidance,—rectification. The fit use of such a man is as hod-man; not feeling the plan of the edifice, let him carry stones to it: if he build the smallest stone, it is likeliest to be wrong, and cannot continue there."

Thus in seeking for the stronghold of order are we constrained before all things and through all things to distinguish the "love" which is "the fulfilling of the law," and which "buildeth up," from the "knowledge" which "puffeth up." "The foundation of God standeth sure;" and as the discipline of obedience indeed keeps pace with the growth of knowledge, we shall prove to ourselves and preach to others that "the work of righteousness shall be peace, and the effect of righteousness quietness and assurance for ever." However fully we may then be aware of the liability of colleagues or of successors to pervert the treasures of knowledge and the outward resources, which they may have shared with us, or shall inherit from us, to unholy ends, we may remember how the prosperity even of a Hezekiah seemed to be in some degree thwarted by the folly of a Manasseh; and conscious of having done what we could, we may with him contentedly query, "Is it not good, if truth and peace be in my days?"

WISH AND WORK.

"I WOULD if I could be as free as the air,
  And as kind as the harvest-moon :
As through the clouds' dance the stars tranquilly glare,
  Through my thoughts would my soul keep tune.

" Life's garden extending beneath my mild sway
  Should be ordered with faultless skill :
Earth's beauties and riches the seasons should lay
  At my feet, to await my will.

" And when the dread crisis arrives, and the earth
  From my converse withdraws its face,
With pious assurance I'd count on the worth
  Of the heavenly store of grace."

But oh ! it were well for thee, offspring of Eve !
  While thy castles in air may stand,
To mark their foundation, and so to believe,
  That thy heart shall sustain thy hand.

Whatever thy fortune, thy hand shall have work :
  Call it labor, or rest, or play,
Thy hand shall find weight, from whose cumber no jerk
  Nor contrivance can break away.

Then work with thy might, as thy soul findeth light !
  It is all that a man can do :
The path of the just may be dim to thy sight,
  But thy work shall refine thy view.

The work of which faith is the wonderful seed,
  As a flower, shall then confess
The reign of that heaven of peace, which hath need
  Of the new earth of righteousness.

THE DISEASE AND THE REMEDY.

"He that believeth shall not make haste." Isa. xxviii. 16.

"FESTINA LENTE—Hasten slowly," is an old motto which is not yet wholly obsolete. It has however, it is to be feared, become to a great extent unintelligible in this age of boasted freedom and expansion. Deliberateness, or thoughtfulness, is indeed the surest guaranty of unfailing promptitude and true expedition; but, now as of old, it is painfully manifest that "haste" and "hurry" are practically almost synonymous terms. We seem ever prone to waste our energies in eagerness, to adopt hurry instead of deliberation as our counselor, and to find ourselves the creatures of flurry and disappointment, instead of the organizers of expedition and success. So will it ever be, with all who forget that the life of a spiritual and rational being depends upon the exercise and repose of faith in "every word that proceedeth out of the mouth of God," rather than upon "the abundance of the things which he possesseth."

So long as we seek our life in material wealth, in physical health, or in social reputation, we must neglect the only source of perfect satisfaction. "Let every man be fully persuaded in his own mind," wrote he who may perhaps pre-eminently be styled the catholic apostle. If happiness be indeed attainable, as Christianity testifies, apart from the fulfillment of any worldly conditions, the true worker will never be tempted to forsake the beneficent career of universal duty, in quest of any local and ephemeral good. Ever directing the eye of his soul upward and onward, he will continually and increasingly

44

outgrow the short-sightedness which is the heir-loom of our nature, and which is accordingly naturally manifested in our undue devotion to the things of earth. His spiritual dignity will show itself in a practical humility, which can joyfully acquiesce in any external allotment of the Supreme Ruler. Being faithful in the " few things," he will indeed in the progress of the Divine economy be made " ruler over more ;" but the reward will be ever attained by a devotion to the incalculable obligations of duty, rather than by a calculating anticipation of the reward itself. Otherwise his work would evidently be one of selfish and therefore rash usurpation, rather than of self-renouncing but safe deliberation. Whatever may be our sphere of action, let us remember that " he that maketh haste to be rich shall not be innocent ;" but that " the liberal man deviseth liberal things, and by liberal things he shall stand."

THE OLD BELL.

Holy bell as ever hung !
　Now again we turn to thee :
Sing the song which erst thou sung
　To our country's infancy !

Dumb no longer mayst thou stand !
　Now anew the strain begin,—
"Liberty throughout the land,
　Unto all that dwell therein !"

Now at length the melter's heat
　Shall thy harmony restore,
While our hearts responsive beat,
　Not with doubtings as of yore.

Doubt and discord brooding then,
　Well thy fortune did relate,
Eloquently mute to men
　Heedless of their high estate.

Now the monsters, with their fry,
　Caste, and truculence, and greed,
In the flaming furnace die,
　And the land afresh is freed.

Broken bell !　In sympathy
　With our crisis and our cure,
Once for all do thou agree
　Gentler burning to endure !

Celebrate the service grand
　O'er our hydra-headed sin,—
"Freedom throughout ALL the land
　Unto all that dwell therein !"

4th and Mo. 1865.

46

PRIMARY PROBLEMS.

---

^ " But I fear lest by any means your minds should be corrupted from the simplicity that is in Christ."—2 COR. xi. 3.

THERE are two queries which continually salute the mental ear of every sensible and earnest man, woman and child, until they find such answers to them as may qualify them to know and do their proper business in the world. The first is, What am I? The second, Where am I? Not until these are answered can we be ready for the farther query, What have I to do?—nor even approach any nearer to it than doubtingly if not miserably to ask, Have I indeed anything in particular to do?

What am I? Our Creator himself mediately tells us that He " formed man out of the dust of the ground, and breathed into his nostrils the breath of life ; and man became a living soul." We do not read that the earth and the waters were commanded to bring forth man, as they were commanded to bring forth the inferior tribes of animated nature. Man has. indeed an animal nature ; and it is even possible that by " the dust of the earth " from which he is so far said to derive his origin, some or all of these inferior tribes may be intended. But it is at least clear that the animal nature is not, never was, and, even in its most refined development, never can be, the man properly so called. It was only " into his nostrils" that " the Lord God breathed the breath of life," and he consequently, and he alone, " became a living soul," however closely those inferior creatures may often imitate the expression of a spiritual life ; or however largely he may himself

5   D   47

sometimes retain the appearance, after having sinfully forsaken the reality, and so become spiritually dead.

It is not necessary for us now to consider particularly the history of the fall of our first parents, and of the salvation which is to be found in Him who is called the Second Adam. It is sufficient for our present purpose to observe that inasmuch as the Soul is the distinguishing principle of manhood, the Body with all its graces and powers is to be viewed as an appendage or parasite to the soul, rather than the soul to it, as we are too apt hastily to assume. The soul is the substance, and the body the shadow, rather than the reverse, as young people especially are in danger of thinking. Let us then consider our first query sufficiently answered, for the present at least, by saying that We are souls.

The next inquiry is, Where are we? To this I think it enough at present to reply, that as souls or spiritual beings, we are each of us in this state of existence tied and confined, more or less closely, to a set of thoughts which we call the mind, which again is tied or confined to the earthen tabernacle which each recognizes as his individual body. It is a solemn truth that we are naturally prisoners; but it is evidently a hopeful alleviation of our fate, that our prison-house is not, except it be by our own choice, the solitary cell of an individual body or an individual mind, but that we are mercifully allowed upon trial the range of the common realm of our fallen nature, and of the earth which partakes of our ancestral curse. In this common prison-house, therefore, as we faithfully explore it for the means of escape, we will be surely privileged to find companionship and sympathy in our search, until all the fetters of individuality and spiritual slothfulness shall be shaken off, by the blessing of God upon our persistent devotion.

The answer to our third query has been thus somewhat anticipated. Our appointed work, we are disinterestedly assured by those who have worked and triumphed before our time, is to glorify God, and to ensure our own eternal happiness by escaping from the bondage of our inherited nature: and that no one may be at a loss for want of explicit direction, each one of us is also commanded, "Whatsoever thy hand findeth to do, do it with thy might." Let us finish our present inquiry with a brief consideration of this ancient text.

"Whatsoever thy hand findeth to do, do it with thy might." All sorts of work, we see, are thus thrown together, and all sorts of people, with the single stipulation that all shall bring earnestness to their work. We are left to infer that by this simple means, confusion and waste of labor will be more surely avoided, than by any amount of anxious contrivance. "Surely," it has been said, "man is a shadow, and life a dream." We so readily forget the evanescence and comparative insignificance of all worldly interests, that we often distinguish and choose too carefully between the different degrees and kinds of knowledge and labor, and may sometimes even exaggerate the diversities of age and station. We are thus apt both to shut our eyes upon the glorious simplicity of all truth, and to lose the strength which is ever to be derived from the essential unity of all true manhood. Let us rest assured that earnest co-operation will always ensure progress, though it be as the corn grows. "a man knoweth not how."

THE RELIGION OF LABOR.

A FAITH in common is a shrine of prayer,
To which true comrades for relief repair,
And banish doubt and disagreement there.

Communities find thus a real bond,
To which all hearts with kindred pulse respond,
And gathered strength, all parted strength beyond.

But private life needs oft its lesser tie—
A bond which infant faith will not supply,
On which each man may constantly rely.

'Tis true, if private faith were clear and strong,
Life would be worship, and its work a song
Which every change of scene would but prolong.

But faith appears to need its time to grow;
And in its non-age will require the show
Of ready forms, through which its force may flow.

Thus then in daily life the need we find
For crude routine, man's purposes to bind
To healthful ways, for body, soul and mind.

Then, with the very reverence of the kirk,
From rude aggression, and from captious quirk,
Protect thy neighbor in his lawful work !

MIND AND MONEY CONSIDERED AS CURRENCIES.

"Happy is the man that findeth wisdom, and the man that getteth understanding; for the merchandise of it is better than the merchandise of silver,
and the gain thereof than fine gold."—PROV. iii. 13, 14.

"Words and money are both to be regarded as only marks of things."—
BERKELEY: *The Guardian*, No. 77.

[NOTE BY THE AUTHOR: I deem it only prudent, in consideration of some
coincidence in the line of argument, to notify the reader that this essay was
written before the appearance in England of the ingenious and learned work
entitled, *The Gay Science*, by E. M. DALLAS.]

THE intelligent observer and actor will hardly need to be
told, in this age of enlightenment, that there are two
principal sorts of currency in the world. By currency I mean,
as everybody means, something which represents wealth or
the objects of enjoyment. Enjoyment, although often itself
loosely spoken of as an object, and pursued as such, and although indeed practically one of the most manifest of realities,
is yet theoretically one of the most indefinable and inscrutable
of mysteries. It is therefore practically, or as an object of
pursuit, identified with those more appreciable and definable
objects of material, moral and spiritual utility, such as physical health, corporeal food and other furniture, social influence,
and personal character, which are the elementary ingredients
of wealth. How far these endowments can justly be regarded
as objects commendable or desirable in themselves, is indeed
a question for moralists to consider, in the investigation of
abstract truth. But until human nature shall be more generally refined to that spiritual and unselfish life which is now

only its occasional and perhaps exceptional aspect, these elementary endowments, it may be assumed, will be the objects rather than the means of its aspirations—its wealth rather than its currencies. It becomes therefore our more immediate duty to acquaint ourselves with the actual currencies or means which practically serve as representatives and vehicles of the recognized wealth which they themselves never are. It must be admitted, indeed, that the materials of currency may become immediate articles of wealth as thus defined; yet as this can only occur and continue while they are withdrawn from use as currency, such a liability cannot vitiate the distinction which is ever obvious to the conscious agent, between his purposed object and his actual means. To be more explicit, therefore, I propose merely to treat of currencies, as currencies.

It appears, then, that the two kinds of currency or means which we have to consider, must resemble one another in having no immediate or intrinsic usefulness or value; but one which depends entirely upon the circumstances that they are, in a mode which only experience can fully explain, a sort of heralds or handles for things which have use or value, and which are wealth. They are alike also in the circumstance that they are both capable of being indefinitely multiplied, and that as it were spontaneously, so that the supply is ever, upon the whole, increased according to the demand, by the very rise of the demand, as well as on the other hand diminished by its decline.—Take these assertions upon faith, for an instant, gentle reader! if some of them appear at first sight to be paradoxical.—They are alike, again, in the circumstance that both may be counterfeited, and so in some degree supplanted by a base currency. They are alike, also, inasmuch as their availability or conventional usefulness appears to be alike dependent upon definite deficiencies in the natural powers of the human race, and therefore alike destined to be limited by the period which shall limit the natural imperfectness of which those deficiencies are a part. There is yet another circumstance of similarity which may seem to have demanded an earlier place in the list; but as I do not attempt to be either complete or very systematic in my account, I will mention it here, at whatever risk of producing it out of due time. This last circumstance is the fact, that although both of them are only known and realized as they may seem to be private property, and are held in the heads or hands of individuals, they are not essentially either of them private property, even while withheld, as they sometimes are under the infatuation of a short-sighted policy, from their proper service as currency; but are even then merely standing, instead of moving representatives, of some form of that true wealth, in the accumulation or command of which alone, private property can consist. Strictly speaking they are both of them, from beginning to end, public institutions, or private only in so far as all public interests may seem to have a private origin and application. Cautious reader! let us pause before proceeding closely to examine these vague enunciations, in order to assure ourselves that we are thinking together upon one ground of thought, and with the same subject-materials.

The two species of currency I am attempting to compare are called severally, Ideas, and Money. Both of them are articles which it may be rather difficult at first thought to define, owing to the reckless manner in which both are tampered with by officious meddlers, or by those who have been taught to think that such meddlings are legitimate and productive branches of industry. These intrusions, however, are in their nature self-limited. A crisis, as it is called, moral or monetary, breaks out from time to time, as sudden, perhaps, and seemingly capricious as a vernal shower, or as a novel freak of Parisian costume, and sweeps the clogging grievances from their nestling-place, almost as kindly as the cleansing stream which glides, impotent for evil, from the plumage of the plunging water-fowl. In general terms, these currencies may both be defined as consisting of certain materials in con-

5 *

nection with certain impressions or patterns which determine
the size and appearance of the material as tendered. The
materials in both cases are in themselves permanent or indestructible, and, as prepared for service, are powerful according
to the amount of weight, physical or metaphysical, which may
be thrown into the pieces at the time of their issue. These
two circumstances are those which are of fundamental importance ; the form of the impressions being in both cases
more or less arbitrary and variable, although it also is adven-
titiously necessary as an intelligible certificate that the whole
thing is actually a piece of currency of a certain value. The
material of the kind which we name Ideas, is crude or latent
Thought : but as the term " Thought" is so commonly used
to signify a defined and transferable idea, it may be well here
to derive another name from its physiological relations, and to
designate this crude material by the name of Brain, with the
proviso that we thereby intend only the element, or quality,
or function of brain, which must be common to all thinkers
who are capable of holding correspondence with each other.
The material for money is not quite so definitely and exclusively provided for man by the hand of the Creator, inasmuch
as this form of currency is not so entirely a Providential and
indispensable institution as the other, having been left more
largely to the ordering of human invention, so that there is
more room for selection from the various materials of nature.
The only materials, however, which we need here note are
those elementary substances which are styled " the precious
metals ;" and of these the metal Gold may be named as a
convenient and here sufficient representative : the rest are too
familiarly known to require any notice now, beyond the remark, that the principles which regulate the employment of
gold as currency, are alike applicable to them as currency,
since they are, so far, nothing more nor less than gold diluted,
as it were, in different degrees of strength.

Patient reader! let us now briefly review and more
particularly consider the points of resemblance, paradox-

ical or not paradoxical, which we lately remarked upon collectively.

First : that of no intrinsic value. Mere brain, and mere gold—alike glittering, it may be, and in their very pliancy tenacious of their native coherency, but intrinsically cold, heavy, lifeless and barren—how impotent of themselves to feed the hungry, to clothe the naked, to shelter the homeless, or to cheer the faint or heal the wounded heart! Little, surely, of confirmation is called for here. The adventitious importance or availability is scarcely even temporarily imparted to the coin concerned in either case, being rather imputed by a necessary submission to the metaphysical unity of the law of perception in the one, and in the other by the voluntary establishment of an artificial uniformity upon the consent of custom. It may seem, indeed, that there here occurs a serious diversity between the two currencies, to the disparagement of the currency of ideas. Thought, as currency, may at first sight seem to be less deserving of attention and care, because it may seem that the portion used is not sacrificed in the using, as is the case with the currency of money. Since the holder or user while conveying it to others appears to retain as much of it as he parts with, or rather to part with none of it, its importance as an object of solicitude may appear to be less urgent inasmuch as the possession of it is thus apparently more secure in its very nature. In other words the communication of thought appears to be different from that of gross matter, and rather like that of flame, in which the lighting of a fresh torch does not extinguish that already burning : whereas in conveying the other kind of currency, whether it be for a satisfactory consideration or not, one wholly relinquishes possession of the amount transferred ; so that this, it may appear, being the only fugitive form of currency, has at least upon that account a positive value, and requires to be guarded with greater vigilance. The comparison thus drawn, however, is unjust; and the appearance a deceptive one. There is a difference in the two cases, but it points in the opposite direction. The real difference, as well as the seeming one, springs from the fact that the currency of money, being once coined, is good for an indefinite period, and for an indefinite number of transactions ; so that that which comes into the hand may serve in the place of that which goes out; while the coin of Thought, having been once used, is thenceforth useless until it shall be again passed through the mint of the brain, except in so far as it may happen to obtain a conventional permanence and value by " passing into a proverb," and so become a specimen of credit-currency comparable to " paper money." As " circumstances alter cases," an apposite idea is (if we may coin a word for the present occasion) *un-coined* by the lapse of the occasion to which it was strictly appropriate, and returned into the bullion-state or raw material of crude thought : and this can be effectually re-converted into the intellectual coin, only at the moment when it is wanted for use, since in that way only can it adequately meet the then present circumstances and obligations, and justly assume the dignity and influence of undoubted currency. While, therefore, the only solicitude needful, in regard to the currency of gold, is, that the agent should keep himself within the region of action in which its motion is indeed one of circulation and not one of mere outflow ; with regard to the currency of brain, there is the additional call for that care in adapting the issue to the occasion, which may make it efficient in all cases precisely according to the demands of the occasion. The importance consequent upon practical fugaciousness is thus really assignable to the currency of mind in a greater degree than to that of money.

Second : that the supply of either currency is simply dependent upon the demand, and as it were produced by the demand.—With regard to the development of mind which constitutes the supply of brain-currency, this position is sufficiently illustrated and fortified by those pioneer, and therefore often forgotten, principles of metaphysics and of common sense ; first, that the actual demand for thoughts on any known subject is the unequivocal expression of a power to produce such thoughts ; and second, that an unknown subject must ever be, at the best, but as a mystical phantom lying out of the reach either of thought or of definite desire, until the mind is placed, so to speak, in a situation near enough and clear enough for its partial or complete apprehension ; that is, until it becomes partly or wholly a known subject.——The adjustment of the supply to the demand of the actual money which for convenience we have styled gold-currency, may be influenced accidentally by extraneous causes, such for example, as the timely expansion of the supply of bullion in our own age : but here as in the former case its own laws are at least generally sufficient for the purpose, although operating somewhat more indirectly than those which regulate the " floating capital " of mind. An increased demand not extraneously provided for, will increase the supply by first reducing the size of coins, so that the conventional value of the whole mass of currency shall be augmented to an equality with the want of the community. Under a decreased demand, this process would of course be simply reversed.

Third : that they may both be counterfeited.—Surely there is nothing paradoxical in this, melancholy as the allegation may well appear ! Base coin is not seldom " uttered " in the place of money :—and still oftener the crude or corrupt conceit of an undeveloped or unsound intellect makes its appearance as a spurious brain-material, which assumes in its outflow such a superficial adaptation to acknowledged needs, or such a vague resemblance to ideal realities, as forms it into deceptive notions—mere notions or counterfeit ideas. Books and banks, it must here be observed, among other links of likeness, are too apt to become the lurking-places and strongholds of the corruptions of currency which ensue in either case, when the means are coveted and cherished as ends.

Fourth : that they are both of only temporary importance.

as being agencies which compensate for imperfections in the
present nature of mankind.—A man's earnings are his wages.
These wages are essentially merely the claims which he has
upon the wealth of the world, for having in some measure
done his duty to the world, as in the sight of the divine
Maker and rightful Master of the world.   Money is originally
valuable to its holder only as being an efficient evidence or
recognized law by which the world at large, so far as he may
be brought into contact with it, is made to perceive and regard those claims until they are fairly met and canceled.
And it remains to be truly valuable under all the sophistica-
tions and perversions of custom, only in so far as it is still
available for this purpose.   It is thus at best a mere substitute,
and too often a lame one, for that clear and honest memory on
the one part, and for that perfect insight and openness on the
other, which would render such a guarantee superfluous by
directly manifesting and promptly ensuring all rightful individual claims.——A man's thoughts as held by memory are
the mere record of the impressions which he has derived and
deduced from his experience in the world, and are accordingly
tinctured with all the imperfections or peculiarities (these
terms being here wholly synonymous) of his powers of observation.   When these disabilities shall be escaped from,
there will be no farther occasion for memory, since he will
see all things and judge all events, which claim his attention, as they really are, without overlooking any of the circumstances or relations which recollection and study are now
called upon to supply so imperfectly.   In other words, thought
and memory will both be lost or merged in pure insight, and
discussion, in pure communion.

Fifth : that they are both public property, and of private
applicability only so far as private interests are tributary to
public interests.—This proposition is obviously to some extent
involved in the one last considered.   Not only, however, is
money originally the silent exponent and passive administrator
of an otherwise latent and abortive law ; but legislation ex-

pressly adopts it as a public institution, by guarding the integrity of the coinage, and by otherwise securing to it that authority which unstudied custom primarily bestows in recognizing the universality of natural rights to the accumulations of actual wealth as private property. The public obligation thus incurred is, indeed, often spurned or slighted by those most nearly concerned, who are apt to be more pleased with the influence so derived, than anxious to appreciate the origin and nature of their title to it. For an authority which is confessedly derived entails the idea of responsibility in some direction, and this is sure to become irksome to capricious tempers. Happily, however, bright examples may almost always be found of the great understanding and the patient spirit* which can cheerfully accept the public rank thus imparted as an occasion of responsibility as well as a means of power.——In the currency of Ideas, as has already been observed, peculiarities are necessarily imperfections, pure thought being wholly impersonal or dividual in its character. It is, indeed, by virtue of its inherent dependence upon the supreme Spirit of Love, at once absolute power and perfect impartiality, and so the very substance and essence of all law. Private interpretation is obviously incompatible with such an institution as this; and the pride of opinion is therefore doubtless yet more insane than the pride of purse.

Prudent reader! let us not rashly descend into the dark mines of subjective research, nor linger too fondly even among the grateful shades and romantic beauties which disguise their dangerous entrance. Let us leave their precious ores and massive realities, with their associated stifling exhalations, to fulfill their own course of secret development and gradual revelation in obedience to the fiat of the all-sustaining and e er-acting Creator; while we devote our powers to our own parts of duty in the more glaring and shifting but living scenes, which are at once the surface, the purpose and the superstructure of those abstract foundations. Nevertheless,

* PROV. xiv. 29.

let us not too timidly turn our eyes from the meagre skeleton of truth which thence bursts forth upon our passing gaze, nor regard it as but the monstrous creature of a dream, or a thing essentially devoid of meaning. Surely, its dead and empty but inexorable form may be a fit memento of the incompetency of the bare laws of matter and of mind to meet the aspirations of the soul! Surely, it points the watchful eye beyond and above these limitations of fate, to such an unselfish rule of enjoyment, as may secure us, through life's protracted crisis and in the mysterious portals of death, from man's extremest and most typical errors, even that of the greedy miser, and that of the groping mystic!

THE AVENUES OF WEALTH.

'Tis vain to seek for source or cause,
Except through avenues or laws :
And still all causes more remote appear,
The more their outward workings are made clear.

'Tis so with wealth ; we seek its source
Most wisely, through its open course ;
From disappointment guarded, when we find
Its seat still baffling the pursuit of mind.

The senses and the appetites
Are simple modes and ready lights,
Through which we well may be content to reach
Such laws of wealth as man to man can teach.

As prime receptacles and guides,
In these earth's happiness resides :
And all the laws their genuine lessons urge,
In guidance to the perfect bliss converge.

Of light, and sound, and form, and space,
One sense * for each conveys the grace
To mind : the rest are but one varied touch,
Which serves the body, not the mind as such.

Their appetites to these belong,
Each fitting each, or weak or strong :
And all the senses join in one, of time,
To which one appetite, for work, must rhyme.

And since the healthy man is one
In what is known and what is done,
By curb and concert all may be controlled,
Save morbid appetites, like that for gold.

* Seeing, Hearing, Grasp, or Co-ordinative Touch, and Muscular Resistance, are here
assumed, as modes of sensation consisting in the communication of the imponderable principles of matter ; as the others, namely, Smell, Taste, and Simple Touch, or Touch Proper,
do, in that of its atomic substance.

THE SURFEIT OF SENTIMENT.

"Then will I turn to the people a pure language, that they may all call upon the name of the Lord, to serve Him with one consent."—ZEPH. iii. 9.

THE readers of a popular magazine * were recently entertained with a satirical article on the subject of bookmaking, entitled "The Cadmean Madness." The force of the argument lay in the present evident tendency of the brainpower of civilization to embody itself in literature, preferentially and preponderatingly over any other mode of expression, and in the absence of any generally observed principle of counteraction and consequent diversion. The most purely intellectual mode of expression being the most inviting for those who are seeking the widest possible audience for intellectual revelations, word-work must with such supplant other sorts of labor to the exact extent in which they may overestimate the importance and novelty of their messages. Thinkers are evidently liable so to overestimate, in proportion as they may fail to appreciate the lasting force of the ancient precepts, that "there is no new thing under the sun," and that "wisdom crieth without; she uttereth her voice in the streets." Forgetting, accordingly, that the object of the advocate of truth is rather to clear his own hands of the blood of all men, than to gain proselytes to any system of doctrinal ideas, like the dog at the river's brink, we are prone to sacrifice certain attainment in catching at imaginary advantage, with no other result than that of disturbing the otherwise placid current of social thought. Past and present experience

* *The Atlantic Monthly*, XIV. 265.

might seem to prove that "all the Lord's people"* cannot
hope to be " prophets," without incurring the fate of the dis-
appointed quadruped, and filling the channels of mental
communication with wasted materials of nutriment.

A little reflection must discover the truth that this is one of
those superficial evils which may be said to cure themselves.
One of the older Biblical books sufficiently indicates the
manner in which, to the end of time, all additions to the revealed code were to be' made. The good word must be
" fitly spoken." Truth is never in such desperate danger
that it is necessary to sacrifice decency for its safety. Adap-
tations of mode, and time, and place, are all essential to a
genuine prophecy. The true teacher of men will no more
cater to popular tastes in his choice of phraseology, than he
will hasten his utterance in deference to current apprehen-
sions of a famine of the Word, or than he will attempt to
reach the antipodes with the sound of his voice. Comparison, that never failing light of worldlings, will clearly enough
and soon enough manifest the difference between the false
teacher and the true ; and the instinctive tendency of every
human soul " to see itself as others see it," will complete the
cure. Let us rest assured that no Malthusian theories are
necessary to stifle the progeny of mind, and that no literature
can permanently prevail which is not built upon " thoughts
t iat breathe," and composed of " words that burn."

* Num. xi. 29.

8 *   E

ECCENTRICITIES.

As springs of action arc the strength of life,
So inward discord fosters outward strife :
The lack of concert in our thoughts and aims
Supports the only grief which rightly shames.

To hopes concentred in the Highest Good,
All scenes and changes lend a genial food,
As ripening ears could erst the hunger stay
Of Truth's disciples plucking by the way.

Upon that Rock of refuge such repose,
From which the crystal current ever flows
Which fills with harmony each faithful soul,
And quickens all into a healthy whole.

Alas ! that such rich boon should e'er be spurned—
That boon on Calvary's height divinely earned
For all who imitate the Heavenly Will
Which wrought its wondrous work by being still.

But since the olden taint infects these frames
Until that miracle their waste reclaims,
The willing spirit may perchance obey
The while the body lingers on the way.

Feelings and powers combined our nature throng ;
Each sense acute implies an impulse strong.
Some strong, some weak, in connate pairs they move,
And all our foibles by their frolics prove.

One finds temptation in the love of smiles ;
Another, meat more readily beguiles ;
One works with words to rivet rules well-known ;
While one may seem to be a faultless drone.

HEALTHY ZEST.

"Whosoever shall not receive the kingdom of God as a little child, shall in no wise enter therein."—LUKE xviii. 17.

"CHILDHOOD and youth are vanity." All the graces of the outward creation, being fugitive in their nature, must ever be sources of disappointment to those whose natural desires are not subjected to that spiritual and self-forsaking faith, by which the precarious enjoyment of the present is made subservient to the sure hope of the future. Only by virtue of the genuine industry which thus begins from within, can the enslaving and separating power of fleshly lust be exchanged for the emancipating and uniting power of spiritual love, and the soul be qualified for communion with the encompassing cloud of witnesses who are secretly exhorting it to "look through nature up to nature's God."

But although childhood or youth is thus necessarily definable as an evanescent and deceptive aspect of life, the revelation of the present unites with the testimony of the past in asserting, that it is upon the whole an enduring and controlling influence. As an aspect of universal nature at least, it is permanent; and no other natural phenomenon is found to embody at once so charmingly and so powerfully, the Divine Wisdom which is both ancient and new. As mankind make the kingdom of heaven the goal of their worldly career, they will doubtless ever have occasion to advert to the language of the latest childhood as one of the latest voices from heaven.

There is in the loose philosophy and theology of childhood, but little of the mystical element which characterizes the more coherent theories of our later years. The creed of boys and girls is prevailingly of a practical cast. The primary power of external perception, which is led by rambling desire and fed by spontaneous sensation, is more vivid with them than the secondary one of ideal comparison, which depends rather upon steadfast attention and deliberate recollection. Abstract principles are by them either unattainable, or are seized with a directness of intuition which the intervention of words could only obscure. What is universally plausible to them, is likely to be indisputably true.

Children are pre-eminently social beings. Their very bashfulness may be regarded as but an expression of their love for the society from which they are morbidly afraid of excluding themselves, by failure in performing their part as members of the social compact. If anything, therefore, in the spontaneous policy of childhood is pre-eminently deserving of consideration by manhood, such must be the rule, if the rule can be found, by which they maintain so largely that pacific, and yet commanding grace of sociability, of which manhood so often and so readily loses, not only the possession, but the appreciation.

There is one, and only one, invariable ground of exclusion from the privileges of youthful society. He who "cannot take fun," and he alone, is the universal outlaw. This is evidently not because children especially delight in inflicting pain or in imputing shame; but because they well know, without an appeal to abstractions, that the maker of sport will make himself more ridiculous than the taker of it, if he forsakes that ground of plausibility to their unsophisticated perceptions, which is generally identical with the ground of truth. The morbidly sensitive culprit is condemned by them, substantially because he prefers a transient and relaxing repose in the hallucinations of self-hood, to the more enduring and invigorating joy which they find upon the field of external nature, in the pursuit of fellowship, if not in the positive sacrifice of self.

It must be acknowledged, however, that even the rule of sociability is one rather of compromise than of comprehension. The fellowship which is not based upon self-sacrificing Love, must originate in a supreme regard for individual comfort, however enlarged may be its appreciation of the natural sources of that comfort. Society, being a sure means of happiness only as it may supply individual deficiency in the pursuit of truth and performance of duty, must disappoint the expectation of those who make it the ultimate object of pursuit. Limiting their aspirations for good by the measure of past experience, such must sooner or later find their moral development outstripped by that of more youthful or more self-sacrificing associates, and become in their turn the objects of reproach or of pity. The pursuit of pleasure even here cannot safely in any degree supplant that of duty. In social converse, as in every other species of occupation, there may be an eager catching at comfort, which must be compensated for by the hearty taking of shame, even though it come in the form of open ridicule or rebuke, before the lover of pleasure can rank with the lovers of truth. Apparent lapses or actual short-comings may occur even in those who have "bought the truth," by reason of constitutional infirmity, as age shall blunt the perceptions and exhaust the powers of body and mind which have been authoritatively and comprehensively characterized as the "earthen vessel," and through which alone the flow of their spiritual life can be manifested to mortal eyes. But although their innocency of purpose may thus fail to prevent inconsistency of conduct, a watchful humility will secure such from surprise and confusion upon the occasion of its exposure; and their steadfast patience will then demonstrate that they have indeed not lost "the dew of their youth." Far otherwise must it be with the unhappy compromisers who are at once unavoidably sensitive to ridicule, and willfully ignorant of those spiritual riches, which infinitely surpass the transferable treasures of intellectual and sensual experience. Anxious, it may be, both to "endure hardness" and to taste pleasure, they can do neither, because their love even of social converse and human approbation, is only another name for selfishness. Having never submitted to the righteous fear which would induce self-denial, and would end in self-sacrifice, they are necessarily strangers to the restoring and sustaining Love which is another name for the Divine Source and Substance of all blessings. Rashly expending the light and life which have been lent to them as an earnest of promised good, in closing the doors and windows of their hearts against the influence of heavenly grace, they are so far necessarily incurring the doom of " the blackness of darkness for ever."

The Light of Divine Love is an all-penetrating as well as an all-powerful agency on behalf of its devoted observers. It is not only their rule of action, but also the rule by which they judge of actions. " He that doeth truth cometh to the light, that his deeds may be made manifest that they are wrought in God." In it alone can we hope fully to harmonize fact with theory. In it the errors and infirmities of the creature will not be allowed to withstand the progress of universal truth, nor the fancied dignity of human character to enter into competition with the glory of the beneficent and omnipresent Creator and Saviour. " Wisdom crieth without, she uttereth her voice in the streets." The inexhaustible treasury of Eternal Truth is ever open to those who bring childlike candor to the work of investigation and demonstration. " In thy light," said the royal Psalmist, " we shall see light." So, in the language of the immediate heir of his dignity and wisdom, " The path of the just is as the shining light which shineth more and more unto the perfect day." So also, the blessed Antitype of all sublunary royalty, who is at once the Captain of Salvation and the Prince of Peace, in his human person enjoined, " Walk in the light while ye have the light, that ye may be the children of the light." Let us also, in contemplation of the almost equal delusiveness and transitoriness of mental and of physical attainments, as compared with the ineffable graces of spiritual life, remember the prayer and injunction of the apostle to the Gentiles, and the warning of the mother of Jesus;—" That God may give unto you the spirit of wisdom and revelation, the eyes of your understanding being enlightened, that ye may know what is the hope of his calling, and what the riches of the glory of his inheritance in the saints." " Charge them that are rich in this world that they be not high-minded, nor trust in uncertain riches, but in the living God who giveth us richly all things to enjoy." " He hath filled the hungry with good things; and the rich he hath sent empty away."

EQUANIMITY.

As sun-down rays seem loosely to ascend
  Expanding from the zenith to the poles,
Anon to stay their flight, and earthward bend,
  Although no earthly tie their course controls;

So human life hath its meridian-line,
  Beyond whose vault the hope may never climb
Of him, who bears not in his heart's design
  The scenes which lie beyond the world of time.

The amplest sky which bounds the worldling's ken,
  Is but the glancing from the general mind
Of that pervading light, in which true men
  Fulfill the high career by God designed.

Its loftiest goal is thus a finite aim :
  A talent buried in the earth, its wealth :
And by its dark horizon veiled in shame,
  Its hopes ambitious disappear with stealth.

And, to the sense which reads them from below,
  Those earnest aspirations show like fate,
By which the freeman seeks all truth to know,*
  And marks its bearing on the world's estate.

But as to eyes with unrestricted reach
  Which could above the mists of earth emerge,
The constant beams another view would teach,
  In that they neither scatter nor converge ;

So can the soul unfettered trace the course
  By which the Christian proves his lifelong aim,
As undisturbed by the degrading force
  Of rash ambition and retreating shame.

* "He will guide you into all truth." JOHN xvi. 13.

THE CRIMINALITY OF COVETOUSNESS.

I DOUBT not that other students of the morality of the
Apostle Paul have felt with me some temporary surprise,
in contemplation of the emphasis with which he condemns
covetousness, as a sin which is not to be named among professing Christians. The ready inference I think is, that he
considered it so glaring a fault, that it should not be even
thought of as a possible thing among such people. After
allowing for the fact that the profession of a spiritual faith
was a less fashionable, and therefore a more significant thing
then than it may now be, I think that others than myself
among the modern readers of the " weighty and powerful
letters," must have been at a loss to appreciate his language
on this subject, so long as they may have regarded the covetousness of that age as identical with the mere desire of pecu-
niary accumulation so common in our own. A slight comparison of the social organization and institutions of these so
distant epochs, must, I think, suffice to suggest a material
change in the meaning of the term.

The simple truth of the matter I conceive to be, that the
" covetousness" of that day was more inseparable from the
taint of jealousy and envy, than is our modern " acquisitive-
ness." Although considerations of worldly wealth then doubtless had a large influence in defining the social position of
individuals, there was not then the same interval which we
now find between the extremes of the social scale. There

7   71

were neither moneyed corporations for the investment and seeming secretion of surplus capital, nor eleemosynary institutions for the systematic support of an outcast, pauper population. Neither redundancy nor destitution seems to have been possible to the extent in which they prevail in our more complicated, if not more artificial, state of society. The money-seeker accordingly had neither the plea which he now finds on the one hand, in the fear of destitution and disgraceful dependence; nor that which is no less certainly, though perhaps more vaguely, presented on the other hand, in the consideration that the mysterious gain which he grasps at is as yet, practically, the property of nobody in particular. To seek for an increase of wealth otherwise than by a direct development of natural resources, was therefore then more obviously than now, to plot to deprive another man of that which was justly his own, without any extenuating pretext of necessity. The only conceivable pretext being the love of social pre-eminence for its own sake, or some still baser desire whose fulfillment must involve manifest loss and consequent degradation to a fellow-being, I cannot avoid the inference that jealousy or envy is really the vice, which, under the name of covetousness, is permanently branded as infamous in the third verse of the fifth chapter of the Epistle to the Ephesians.

INTEREST.

TRUE language is a valid thing
　To him who cares to know it,
Making the very parrot sing,
　And seem to be a poet.

But emptily, or shamefully,
　The forms of language flourish,
For him who will not deign to see
　The lessons they would nourish.

His dictionary binding him
　With literal injunctions,
He counts it but an idle whim,
　That speech hath living functions.

To some words, such as Interest,
　He finds a plural meaning;
And grieves that things are ill-exprest,
　Though loth to seem o'er-weening.

Ah no! let none be over-wise!
　Much wisdom knows much sorrow.
But still, 'twere well some small supplies
　To own, where none can borrow.

And Interest means, a profit pure;
　The food of strength and beauty;
An income from investment sure;
　A consequence of duty.

All interest is and ever shall
　Be one, as thus we learn it;
And principle and principal
　May well unite to earn it.

CHRISTIAN OPTIMISM.

"According to your faith be it unto you."—MATT. ix. 29.
"These things have I spoken unto you . . . that your joy might be full."
—JOHN xv. 11.

THE famous maxim of Aristotle, that "Nature abhors a vacuum," may be regarded as the nearest substitute which his sagacity could supply for the simple and sublime doctrine of the omnipresence of God in nature.

Physics and Metaphysics.

The atmosphere was not indeed unknown to him; but being known only upon the principle of comparison as an element of unbounded freedom, he could not readily conceive of its being subject to any principle of constraint within itself. It was even occasionally regarded in the elaborate but loose system of Grecian mythology, as the very embodiment of the Supreme Being. The idea of its being a passive subject of mechanical force is plainly irreconcilable with a view which exalted it to the dignity of an abstract law, if not to a divine independence of law.

It was thus that this master of physical philosophy accounted in the realm of physics, for the universal phenomenon of all existence, that capacity implies craving. The more inveterate difficulties of metaphysicians in defining the fundamental principles of their science, seem to have originated in a somewhat similar mode; the principal difference lying in the accession of an independent will to the dependent capacity, and the consequent complication of all subordinate phenomena. Consciousness, apart from volition, is evidently

74

nothing more than the satisfaction or disappointment of a craving capacity. It is the co-existence therewith of a will, or power of election which constitutes the conscious subject an influential agent, responsible, under God, to himself and to other intelligences for his use of that will.

The course, if not the source, of modern metaphysical and theological controversy is well illustrated in the different constitutions of the English and German national minds, as revealed in some discordancies in the national languages. Versatility of Faith, as the principle of progress. In the English tongue the word Faith is not always synonymous with the word Belief, being distinctively applied to the conventional idea of a scriptural meaning of the original Greek term, different from, and possibly opposed to, any belief which can arise independently of written revelation. The German mind appears to be either incapable of adopting this development of doctrine, or to reject it as a mere technical redundancy. So far as revelation may be regarded as an ever new experience, practically limited only by the incapacity of its recipients to appreciate its omnipresent and otherwise omnipotent Source, the German usage is evidently preferable on the grounds of independence and simplicity. The German tongue also ignores the English distinction of the scriptural " miracle," from the colloquial " wonder." Possibly both distinctions may have originated in an excessive deference, on the part of the less speculative nation, to the cautionary precept of the learned apostle, " not to think above that which is written." Surely it must be a servile, and in the end a suicidal, deference, which would identify the writing with the thing written. The one is but the visible sign ; the other is the invisible but multiform substance. It is evidently this substance which the inquirer is cautioned against disregarding, upon the simple ground that inconsistency proves error. Capriciousness must be excluded ; but versatility, being essential to faith as the secret principle of formal development or obvious progress, is not only compat-

7*

ible with, but is actually inseparable from, the maintenance of spiritual truth ; and the very literalists who thus oppose it, most evidently condemn themselves in the thing which they allow.

Faith definitely, or objectively, identical with Volition, "Hast thou faith? Have it to thyself before God. Happy is he that condemneth not himself in that thing which he alloweth."* All safe theorizing concerning life and happiness must begin with the duties and demands of the individual man. An independent faith is the only faith which is scripturally endorsed as a consistent and saving faith. When, accordingly, we consider the fewness of the elements which enter into an ultimate analysis of human nature, and the radical importance of faith as a principle of conduct, it becomes difficult to affix any universal value to that term, which may not be equally well conveyed by the more familiar term Belief, or the more precise term Volition. If belief in conception, or volition in action, be in all cases a mere act of election between competing spiritual influences, its only independence must lie in the circumstance, that the submission of the agent is self-directed. Arrogance is plainly precluded by such a view, and responsibility is not ignored. If the power of divine inspiration can be thus certainly admitted and secured as the animating principle of characters which are most complicated in the details, and most diversified in the peculiarities, of their constitution, what need have we to seek for any farther definition of faith, or any farther explanation of its ever miraculous efficacy? If truth is one and all-satisfying in its nature, and the power of apprehending it thus open to all mankind, is not every capacity and every craving, both of the individual and of the social nature in all men, abundantly provided for? What remains for any to do in their own behalf, but to "seek God while He may be found," to "call upon Him while he is near," and to "resist the Devil" that he may "flee from" them?

<hr>

* Rom. xiv. 22.

Let us however be always ready to prove
our faith by "that which is written." The and Religion, with Science.
true fossils of language testify distinctly to the
unity, and permanence, and ever-progressive development of a
divine plan in the ordering of human affairs; and their testimony to that effect is more important and more eloquent than
that of geological revelation as to the history of the material
world, by as much as the life of conscious mind is more noble
than that of vegetative growth and of brute instinct. Witness
the word of the ancient prophet* upon the true development
of faith in works, and the practical spirituality of the lesson
of life. "Wherewith shall I come before the Lord, and bow
myself before the high God? Shall I come before Him with
burnt offerings, with calves of a year old? Will the Lord be
pleased with thousands of rams, or with ten thousands of
rivers of oil? Shall I give my first born for my transgression, the fruit of my body for the sin of my soul? He hath
showed thee, O man, what is good; and what doth the Lord
require of thee, but to do justly, and to love mercy, and to
walk humbly with thy God?" The doctrine of the native su-
periority of the soul is implied in the very idea of its existence, since the very rudest conceptions of an invisible world
must be confirmed, if not suggested, by the observed incompetency of material phenomena to govern even themselves.
The responsibility for sin, in and through the consequent
consciousness of shame in the sinner, is the secret source of
all the false doctrines of Atheism and Materialism. By shut-
ting our eyes to the light of the spiritual world, we may temporarily ignore its existence, and suppress the alarm of a dis-
turbed conscience. But the cravings of an immortal nature
will not the less continue to be felt, and as the inevitable consequence of our self-imposed limitation we will then seek to
satisfy them with the beggarly elements of outward experience. Thus with a rebellious resistance to the divine authority of Truth as measurably manifested in the law of con-

* MICAH vi. 6, 7, 8.

science, the very possibility of contentment is destroyed, and the willful transgressor becomes a willful complainer. The denial of responsibility, he finds, will not save him from the fate of suffering. He has no hope of happiness, save in retracing the wanderings of his will, as the despised and rejected "Sun of Righteousness" may still at his cry arise in his conscience "with healing in his wings." So, learning to regard the soul as the appointed custodian of his outward life, he will not only have to acknowledge that it has been the subject of sin and the seat of suffering; but also that, as the body is "brought under and kept in subjection" it is redeemed from the power of the spiritual enemy, who can beset it only through the infirmity of the flesh, and made a partaker of that kingdom which "is righteousness and peace, and joy in the Holy Ghost."

"What I must do," writes a cotemporary
Resulting assurance. teacher,* "is the question which concerns me, and not what the people think." May we so keep the first principles of experience ever in view, as to be able not only to consult them readily in the determination of our own career, but to appeal to them boldly in demonstration of the hope which is in us, at whatsoever risk of being charged with offensive dogmatism by caviling critics! If we have any thing to say, let us pass by the complainers, and address ourselves to the inquirers as those with whom we are more likely to communicate to mutual advantage. "We cannot but speak the things which we have seen and heard," was the testimony of Peter and John to the Jewish rulers who imprisoned and threatened them. "And now, Lord, behold their threatenings, and grant unto thy servants that with all boldness they may speak thy word," was the prayer of the Church when exulting over their release. "Finally, brethren," wrote Paul to the Thessalonians, "pray for us that the Word of God may have free course and be glorified . . . for all men have not faith." And again, to the Romans, "The

* RALPH WALDO EMERSON.

Word of God is nigh thee, even in thy mouth and in thy heart; that is the Word of faith which we preach." As true love smites but to heal, and as true hope anchors but to secure, so true faith binds but to emancipate from that lingering bondage to " the weak and beggarly elements," * from that still unmortified " body of death,"† which alone hinders the individual members of the militant Church from realizing in their several measures, " the fullness of Him that filleth all in all."‡

* GAL. iv. 9.   † ROM. vii. 24.   ‡ EPH. i. 23.

F

WELFARE.

THIS world's a world of work, we know.
    Who are not boys,
But seek a life beyond its dancing show
    And thoughtless noise.

We know the envied scene and scope
    Which wealth supplies,
At best are but decoys, that gild with hope
    Life's sacrifice.

That earnest hope may we pursue,
    Or. here, or there,
Which holds our life's realities in view
    By watchful prayer !

Regarding too each brother's path
    And single aim,
Who finds in freely losing all he hath,
    All he can claim.

So may our lives of rectitude
    A chart produce,
Which shall by after-comers be reviewed
    For blessed use.

And as the gentle seasons roll
    Their course of praise,
Dispensing to mankind, from pole to pole,
    Good nights and days ;

May we, responsive to their round,
    Our learning tell,
That they who are to duty's orbit bound
    Always fare-well !

THE COURT OF FORTUNE.

BY the happy ordination of Divine Providence, falsehood can never so far gain currency in the world, as to form part of the constitution of language. To every word there is some legitimate meaning. It is by perverting it from this meaning alone that we can be guilty of neglecting "the form of sound words." It may even be doubted whether any words are at all times more liable than any others to be perverted to the purposes of falsehood, although such occasional liability under the variable bias of public sentiment, is a most obvious index of the tendency of the social mind at particular epochs.

Among the words which in our age are perhaps most likely to be thus perverted, are the nearly or quite synonymous terms, "fortune," and "chance." So familiar have these sounds become as a refuge of unbelievers in the Divine government of the world, that the advocates of truth are sometimes tempted to exclaim, "There is no such thing as chance." Surely, it is merely a limitation of their own vision which prevents them from adding, "except in subordination of an intelligent Providence." Surely it may be nothing worse than a still more narrow limitation of vision which enables their seeming adversaries to imagine not only a chance, but a blind chance. For any present time and occasion the Deity is such as He then and there reveals Himself, however harsh or however partial such revelation may be by comparison with his essential attributes. This is an adaptation which is simply neces-

sary in condescension to our erring or limited powers of intelligence.   To this purport are the words of the prophet-
king, "The Lord hath recompensed me according to my
righteousness; according to my cleanness in his eye-sight.
With the merciful Thou wilt show Thyself merciful, and with
the upright man Thou wilt show Thyself upright.   With the
pure Thou wilt show Thyself pure, and with the froward
Thou wilt show Thyself unsavory." *   There is doubtless such
a thing as chance or fortune in the experience of bewildered
souls, even if they be not hopelessly benighted.   Nothing but
the inward light of grace, can thoroughly reveal the outward
course of Providence ; and until we can profess its clear guidance, let us not indiscriminately decry the vicegerency of
Fortune, however justly we may occasionally protest that we
thereby mean the Power of Providence.   As all earthly institutions are the temporary abodes of power, there is one
institution which may be said pre-eminently to claim the title
of the Court of Fortune.

It is a common saying that they who have taken upon themselves the responsibilities of matrimony, have given "pledges
to fortune."   It is evident that they make themselves increasingly answerable to the community for their conduct, and increasingly dependent upon its indulgence for everything which
may be called a "breach of the peace."   They assume an
obvious external dignity, which is to be secured only by the
support of an internal intelligence, or by a careful subordination to other dignitaries who are possessed of such intelligence.   The love of truth as the source of order, will make
them independent dignitaries ; or the love of order as distinguished from truth, may make them for a while dependent
dignitaries : but in matrimony, as in every other realm of life,
integrity of purpose must confer a dignity of some degree, the
obvious want of which must eventually cover with shame the
reckless adventurer in its domain.   By entering into the married state an individual so manifestly publishes his incompe-

* 2 SAM. xxii. 25–27.

tency for an independent life, that it is difficult indeed to imagine another court in which he can be bound in so heavy a bail " to keep the peace." Opportunities, also, here so coincide with interest, that the preservation of social harmony may be said to be pre-eminently the function of the married portion of the community.

If the keeping of the peace be thus the great business of matrimony, must not every motive thereto be a deceptive and injurious one, which does not originate in the comprehensive disinterestedness of unselfish love? How especially important is it that they who are contemplating an entrance upon its distracting cares, should first carefully study in all things " the form of sound words," with a view to the proper restraint of that member which is so easily " set on fire of hell," and which then " setteth on fire the course of nature !" No otherwise can they hope to realize that serviceable fortune, which will not only be a permanent protection to themselves, but which may increasingly qualify them on all occasions to

> " assert eternal Providence,
> And justify the ways of God to men."

8

THE RISK OF RANK.

A PRETTY thing appears subordination,
   Not to speak of its practical use :
And yet the seeming consequence of station
   Is the source of its common abuse.

The fact is clearer than its rationale :
   For the top of a pyramid crests
The joints below, as worthily as gayly,
   While it shields them from incident pests.

But could that top, while rigid to its level,
   Be seen sidewise to swerve from its place,
It might display the work of self or Devil
   In this marvel of human disgrace.

From base to summit union would suffer,
   And an open discordance ensue,
When winds, erewhile quiescent, give a rougher
   Intimation of what they can do.

And could the parts speak freely with each other,
   With the prior proviso of thought,
The great man's contest with his humbler brother
   Might be then in their dialogue fought.

How rails the recreant block at those below it,
   For conspiring their lord to debase !
And how he deems they yet more plainly show it,
   By pretending to know their own place !

Might some good angel timely teach him reason,
   By reminding how they were secured
Alike from object and success in treason,
   Had they only a monarch ensured !

THE RHETORIC OF RIDICULE.

"In malice be ye children, but in understanding be ye men."—1 Cor. xiv. 20.

R IDICULE may be regarded as the last resort of rhetoric. The famous Grecian expounder of ideal philosophy, whose familiarity with the laws and powers of rhetoric has perhaps never been surpassed save in the person of Him who "spake as never man spake," writing in the name of his equally famous master, thus defines the province of its operation: "Rhetoric is of no use to us for defending our own injustice, or that of our friends or our country. We ought on the contrary to accuse ourselves in the first instance, and next our relatives and our friends, and not to conceal our transgressions, but bring them to light, that we may suffer punishment, and be restored to health; not caring for the pain, but if we have merited stripes, giving ourselves up to the stripe; if imprisonment, to the prison; if death, to death; and employing rhetoric for the accusation of ourselves and of those who are dear to us, that their guilt may be made manifest, and that they may be freed from the greatest of evils, that of injustice." *   We may perhaps now conveniently comprise the same view in fewer words by saying, that it is the province of rhetoric to subordinate personal peculiarities to universal principles, by supplanting the capriciousness of falsehood with the uniformity of truth.

Principles are indeed the mighty materials with which alone the rhetorician must seek to work; but inasmuch as

* PLATO: *Gorgias.*

convincement is his aim, persons also must be the subjects of his operation so far as they are the objects which may be impressed by the application of principles. So long as the circumstances and disposition of the hearer may be equally favorable with those of the speaker for the appreciation of any principle of truth which they may be engaged in investigating, personal considerations may be wholly neglected. But where there is any disparity in these advantages, the parties will of course not see eye to eye; and he who is conscious of seeing or comprehending something more than his associate is able to acknowledge, will be in a corresponding degree qualified to suggest to him the occasion of his lack of vision. So long as this lack can be accounted for by the difference of mere circumstances, the advocate of truth may still supply it under the evident guidance of principles, by demonstrating that difference, and by urging the influence of the subsidiary principles, which the circumstances in question may represent, upon the main topic of discussion. But when he finds, upon thus leading his professed associate, as it were, all around their subject, that there are any aspects from the appreciation of which he invariably shrinks as one dazzled with an excess of light, he has no other alternative than to infer that the difficulty lies in the inherent inconsistency or incompleteness of his companion's nature. He is compelled to decide that he is not wholly a lover of light, and in the fraternal endeavor to correct his misapprehension, will encourage him to such a right exercise of his senses, as shall qualify them "to discern both good and evil by reason of use." His only remaining means to this end will be the exposure, in the clearest light which he can command, of the inconsistency or incoherency of his comrade's views and professions, and so far he will have to descend from the clear sky of principles into the cloudy region of personalities. His work is still, however, not a hopeless one, since the vice of disposition may merely amount to such an habitual prejudice of mind as is comparable to a merely functional and temporary weakness of bodily sight. If the inquirer be so sound at heart as to be advancing in his love for the truth, and "growing by the sincere milk of doctrine," he will patiently endure, and will eventually rejoice over, the transient mortification and exposure which are the means of enlarging his sphere of life and labor in the truth. He will be convinced and will not need to be convicted. He may be a temporary subject of the rule of ridicule, but he cannot be called its victim.

Far otherwise must it be with all who stubbornly close the eyes of their mind to the shining of the divine Light of truth. For such the herald of truth will sooner or later receive the command, "Cry aloud, spare not." As happened in olden time, they will ever be prone to account themselves the monopolists of truth, and to fortify themselves in their own conceit with all the resources of reason and all the sanctions of tradition. But as they persist in their practical denial of the omnipresence of the divine Enlightener and Leader and Feeder of souls, they must necessarily fall into the unpardonable sin of arrogating to themselves the attributes of God. Presuming upon past attainments, and basing their views of merit upon the deceitful ground of human comparison, their shameless assurance can be shaken by but one species of argument. Having abandoned the rule of harmony for that of discord, they are fit subjects for the law of contrast, and the so-called *argumentum ad hominem* becomes applicable to them, as being nothing more nor less than an exposure of the contrast between their profession and their practice. It is an exposure which may be both appreciable in itself, and intensified by reflection from the perception of surrounding beholders. It was with the *argumentum ad hominem* that Elijah discomfited the prophets of Baal previously to their utter extermination; and with it the Redeemer of men condescended to expose the self-righteousness of officious and caviling tale-bearers. As its penalty is originally incurred by a desertion of principles, so its terrors must increase with the progress of selfish transgression, until the rule of ridicule may be overtaken and justly supplanted by that of the unqualified and unsympathizing pity, which is but another name for a righteous contempt. In conformity with apostolic doctrine the unhappy victim may then be charitably neglected as one who is beyond the reach of rhetoric.

Prophecy may be the language of the perfected Christian, but the partial modes of utterance which the Apostle Paul distinguished by the name of tongues must thus still have their place in an imperfect world, as "a sign, not to them that believe, but to them that believe not." "There are, it may be, so many kinds of voices in the world, and none of them is without signification. . . . Wherefore, brethren, covet to prophecy, and forbid not to speak with tongues."

THE MISSIONARY.

WHO shall the willing witness be
To sound the gospel mystery?
Who, with the standard pure unfurled,
Will preach the grace that saves the world?

What, thinkest thou, awaiteth thee
Who sayest, "Here am I, send me!
The fields are white, the hands are few;
And work is pleasure in my view."

Thy path so plain—thy crown so sure—
Thou seemest eager to endure
The cross of care and brunt of strife,
In harvesting eternal life.

Go forth! But, with "the things behind,"
Leave not that discipline of mind
Which is begun when faith begins,—
The timely rod for secret sins!

Regardful of those inner deeps
Where every infant giant sleeps,
Thence never wholly to depart
Till rules the gospel all thy heart;

And conscious there by sympathy
Of every brother's misery,
Acquit thee, through life's shifting scene,
As follower of the Nazarene!

And while thy labors outward flow,
And words or acts thy message show,
Thy all-sufficient guerdon be,
To rise with Him who died for thee!

CUI BONO?

"No truth from Heaven descends upon our sphere,
  Without the greeting of the skeptic's sneer;
  Denied and mocked at, till its blessings fall,
  Common as dew and sunshine, over all."
                                        WHITTIER.

THE vanity of all things is the text both of the skeptic and of the believer. The difference between them is, that the one "utters all his mind," while the other "keepeth it in till afterward," ever retaining his hold on the material of thought, which is the determining principle of utterance. The skeptic claims only to live in the apparent facts of communicable or demonstrable experience, while the believer knows that the roots and fruits of his experience reach beneath and beyond all that can be narrated to his fellow-man. What have you been living for? What has all your labor amounted to? are therefore the questions which they are alike prone to address to their fellow-men, when seeking to lead them to their own way of feeling and thinking, in view of the obvious variance of their practice. Each, as judged by the standard of the other, must obviously be guilty of a sort of continual suicide.

Happily, the belief in an internal existence is identical with that in an eternal existence. In accordance with the proverb "the end crowns all," the true believer knows that the end of all things, so far from being the annihilation of life, is its consummation. By way of setting forth the futility of even the present efforts of his gainsayer, he can not only ask him, What has all thy labor amounted to?—but, What is it all amounting to? If the door of inquiry be thus opened for the entrance of substantial argument, he may proceed to testify, that it is even in vain to query what any previous labor has amounted to, save in so far as the gift of insight and forecast may qualify us in the first place to assert what would have been, had our course been different. The skeptic by ignoring such qualification is indeed enabled to ridicule the believer; but he purchases his temporary impunity at the expense of his own voluntary blindness.

The stronghold of skepticism is thus its inevitable grave Living in surfaces, it can judge only by the comparison of outward experience. Its preponderating regard for the present as masked by the material, renders it proportionally forgetful of the monitions of the past, and blind to the dawn of the future in the light of the spiritual. Counting itself practically wise, it rushes upon that living death of ignominy, in which the loss of the last vestige of respect from once kindred souls converts even the stimulating appearance of present hostility into the withering reality of distant pity. The query, "*Cui bono?*" if it then shall occur to its miserable victims, can only occur in connection with the ironical response of the self-questioning seer, *

"Men may live fools, but fools they cannot die."

* YOUNG: *Night Thoughts.*

TRUTH.

FUTURITY were ever present,
　Were all the present but revealed.
Adversity were not unpleasant,
　Were Truth's resources not concealed.

There is indeed a veil of Isis,—*
　A veil which needs but to be rent,
To manifest in every crisis
　The floods of light in darkness pent.

And in the true crusader's struggle
　There is indeed a force revealed,
By foes esteemed an idle juggle,
　Which serves its friends as sword and shield.

Then rend the veil, and read the battle,
　Whoe'er thou art that lackest aught!
And light and life, and needful chattel
　By hidden Wisdom shall be brought.

On every side see wiles Satanic
　Conducting schemes for future bane,—
For churchman's feud, for merchant's panic,
　For statesman's fall, for all men's pain!

And see through all, one wide endeavor
　To break the rule of reck and ruth,
With stubborn treason prating ever,
　"There's no coherency in truth!"

Through past and present, the hereafter
　Shall shine on thee, whoe'er thou art,
Who bravest strife and scorn and laughter,
　To prove the lessons of thy heart.

* "I am all that was, and is, and shall be; nor my veil, has it been withdrawn by
—*Inscription in temple of Isis.*

FUNGUS AS A WORD.

"The fruit of the Spirit is gentleness."—GAL. v. 22.

WORDS are things. I do not like the word "bloat." As an instrument of language, it seems to me that the thing is either worn out, or in need of repair. If so it may well be released for a time from active service, in order that, like the fallow field of the husbandman, it may renew its strength by an undisturbed exposure to the ceaseless oscillations of upper and of nether elemental influence; or that, like the precious material of his recent manure heap, by the resolution of its offensive ingredients, it may as the pure nutriment of truth recover its efficacy as a constituent in the living machinery of mind. We tend to extremes in all our policy. In language the tendency is shown in the fatality by which words originally indifferent in their moral application acquire a meaning which is either obviously opprobrious or obviously laudatory. The phenomenon of nature which has been once used by the original thinker and speaker as a sign for the expression of dispassionate thought, is quickly borrowed by those who are unable or unsolicitous to distinguish between its abstract value and its personal application; the sentiment is associated with the surroundings; and the epithet or the term, instead of being the channel of useful evidence or of convincing proof, becomes with them that of idle personality or of impotent judgment.

Some words appear to be more liable than others to this exhaustion or corruption of their original value. Metaphors

which may have been derived from the animal kingdom a
more readily received and literalized in an unduly offensi
or flattering signification, than those which have been suppli
by the more obviously unconscious phases and involunta
actions of vegetable life, or by the purely mechanical pl
nomena of inanimate nature. What we call bloating or pa
pering in the animal kingdom, is suggestive of evil agen
because it can only occur in the experience or under t
management of him who is the responsible head of the a
mal kingdom, and in subjects which, exhibiting more or l
appearance of volition and intelligence, are so far apparen
responsible for the maintenance of their own infirmities. T
suggestions, indeed, which must often undesignedly atte
upon the exhibition of facts, may be useful, like shado
upon the ground, as indications to those who cannot lift th
eyes to the contemplation of substances; but inasmuch as t
object of honest speaking is to deal only with facts and all
suggestions to take care of themselves, the honest speaker w
endeavor to use such facts in the illustration of his thought
shall compel the hearer to look upward, or to see nothir
Being himself guiltless of regarding appearances as anythi
more than ambiguous indications of the course of inward li
he will carefully avoid such forms of expression as might le
other observers to accept them as definite manifestations
the secrets of character. Under the guidance of the catho
charity which is able to " believe all things," he will esca
both the reality and the permanent appearance of judging
spiritual dispositions from physical habits. We may thus
think, well prefer the vegetable word Fungus, to the anin
word Bloat, in treating of the moral and mental extravagan
which are so sure to overtake communities who, having lo
reposed in the dense luxuriance of worldly prosperity, ha
insensibly secluded themselves from the unobstructed illur
nation and vigorous ventilation of universal truth.

Words are not things. Nature is the great storehouse
language, as well as of all other worldly wealth. Every me

ing which has not the warrant of an analogy derived from the
universal and mysteriously consistent system of natural truth,
is a fiction of the individual or associate mind, which, when
its value is fairly put to the test, will be found as uncurrent in
the realm of pure knowledge, as is the certificate of an ex-
ploded bank in a community which trades upon credit, or as
is the conventional coin in a district wherein gold is more
abundant than bread. Trust is indeed a glorious and life-
sustaining reality; but even in the use of words it has no
other security than the immutability of truth. As a mere
species of currency, language is at the best but a convenient
abstraction which can and must be adapted at will to every
diversity and contrariety of circumstances. That language is
originally void of objective value, is shown by the original
need of objective illustration and implicit trust in its employment.

The solution of the paradox is a simple one. Nature, as
the work or expression of God, is infinite. Language, as that
of man, is finite. Fungus and Bloat, as terms of substantive
meaning, are, after all, identical if intelligently defined and
trustfully received. The spiritual realm being recognized as
the only sphere of consciousness and independent action, the
animal and vegetable kingdoms of life-manifestation become
essentially one, their long sought dividing-line being found to
have, in nature as in mind, no other than a hypothetical existence. The two words may doubtless be used indifferently
to indicate the superficial depravity of development, in which
quantity usurps the place of quality ; and which, having been
introduced by sin, may be prolonged, although not perpetu-
ated, by an innocent ignorance, in a world abounding with
materials, under the government of Him who "openeth his
hand and satisfieth the desire of every living thing," "who
maketh his sun to shine upon the evil and upon the good, and
sendeth his rain upon the just and upon the unjust."

9   G

MIGHT *vs.* RIGHT.

"GET what you can, and keep what you get!
    Who can be always in search of the right?
Dream what you will of mercy or debt,
    Who can contend with the kingdom of might?

"Welcome such rest as mortals can find!
    Welcome the clouds, for the sake of such light!
Cherish the bonds which righteously bind,
    Satisfied simply that might shall be right!"

Such the advice their learning affords,
    Who, in such station as falls to their lot,
.Cling to the world, and think to be lords
    In their own right, over that they have got.

Slaves to a passing system of things,
    Vainly they struggle that all shall be so,
Craving the comfort company brings,
    Rather than hoping their fate to forego.

Might is to right as body to soul :
    Why need we utter such simple advice!
Charity spreads its living control ;
    Selfishness wastes like the victualler's ice.

Leaving itself, as known by the flesh,
    Charity looks for its objects abroad,
Seeking its life by truth to refresh,
    Shunning like death the contagion of fraud.

Selfishness shrinks from destined decay,
    Nursing the form which the spirit has quit.
Wisdom descends to lighten our way—
    Wisdom's the great matter, therefore get it!*

* PROV. iv. 7.

CHRISTIAN COMMUNISM.

"God is in the generation of the righteous."—Ps. xiv. 5.
"As thou, Father, art in me, and I in thee, that they also may be one in us."—JOHN xvii. 21.

CHRISTIANITY and Fraternity may be said to be synonymous terms in so far as they alike imply the primary relation of Sonship. The true brotherhood which is involved in a conscious reliance upon the Universal Father who is Himself greater than all his works, inhales a freedom and exhales a love which set at defiance every barrier of outward inequality. "Liberty, Equality, and Fraternity" in all the essentials of existence, are still the heirloom of "the multitude of them that believe." Only by the imperfection of belief are any ever excluded from the felicity of being "of one heart and of one soul," and of having "all things common." As belief in the all-convincing Light is ready and persistent, realization of the all-sufficing Good will be full and permanent, however the capacity and sphere of service and enjoyment may vary in various individuals. "These things have I spoken unto you," said the Saviour, "that my joy might remain in you, and that your joy might be full." "Ask in my name and receive, that your joy may be full."

The interior conflict between the rule of Divine Grace and that of morbid sentiment is outwardly reflected in the apparent confusion between the just administration of Providence and the reckless usurpation of Mammon. As, however, the Prince of Peace, who, in his first or historical and yet typical coming, declared that every true follower should be his

" mother and brother and sister," shall be so welcomed in his
second or mystical, and yet individual and most experimental
coming, as to be indeed " formed in us," we cannot but realize both internally and externally that the so-called " Over-
Ruler" is to us through all events, the only actual Ruler.
As this may become our experience, no Satanic subtilty can
so corrupt us " from the simplicity that is in Christ," as to
destroy the blessed assurance, " All things are yours, and ye
are Christ's, and Christ is God's."   Still indeed, while individuality shall endure the desire of communion will remain
as the occasion for the profitable precept, " Let every one of
us please his neighbor for his good to edification ;" but the
blunders of sentiment, and the outrages of avaricious lust can
be effectually combated by no display of words which is not
derived from the " first and great commandment" of the Divine
Man, and from " the second" which " is like unto it."
" Thou shalt love the Lord thy God with all thy heart, and
with all thy soul, and with all thy mind."   " Thou shalt love
thy neighbor as thyself."   The worship which is manifested
by perseverance in enlightened self-interest is the road to that
purity of heart in which all may " see God," and all fragmentary and seemingly conflicting interests be blended and
consolidated in one.

POLICY.

THAT of "Given an inch and extorted an ell,"
Is a trouble earth's rulers have often to tell.
In the worth of experience all men agree:
May experience profit the powers that be!

The display of their strength, and the guard of their dues,
If too often the themes on which potentates muse,
Must result in the loss of both power and means;
For the world travels onward while self-hood o'erweens.

The regarding of self, in the high or the low,
Draws the curse of inaction wherever they go—
The neglect of the work to repose in the way,
While the multitude presses; for all cannot stay.

Every man is a monarch who keeps his true place
As a part of the whole, with discretion and grace.
By discretion in council, and grace in affairs,
He will gain while he gives, and preserve for his heirs.

Every man is a slave who is dead to the ties
By which all, who observe them, in concert will rise.
As his giving or getting is out of their course,
No pretension of zeal shall delay his remorse.

He who yields in the self-hood not only gives worse,
But his blindness thus leads him himself to disburse:
Then, with character lessening, must lessen his dues,
With demands unabated which all men refuse.

So, to get what they can and to keep what they get,
Is the crown of their life who make duty their debt:
But its price and its proof is the will to believe
That to give is more blessed than e'en to receive.

9 *

BIBLIOLATRY AND PANTHEISM.

"In philosophy, men have abused the code of natural, as in theology, the code of positive revelation; and the epigraph of a great Protestant divine on the book of Scripture, is certainly not less applicable to the book of consciousness:

> "*Hic liber est in quo quærit sua dogmata quisque;*
> *Invenit, et pariter dogmata quisque sua.*"

> "This is the book where each his dogma seeks,
> And this the book where each his dogma finds."
>
> SIR WM. HAMILTON.

THE sentiment of a contemporary poet,*—

> "Thought lies deeper than all speech;
> Feeling, deeper than all thought;"

although doubtless liable to obscuration at the hands of hasty creed-builders, is sufficiently clear to the unsophisticated explorer of actual life. Language, articulate or inarticulate, is undoubtedly symbolical and representative in the first place of distinct or indistinct ideas, and, in connection with them, the vehicle of feeling, at least so far as feeling may be communicated from man to man by natural means. The springs of life are evidently hidden deeply beneath the animal senses, and still more deeply beneath the facts of external nature with which those senses are conversant, and which furnish the materials of language. Language, therefore, although in its origin a superficial gift or invention, is in its efficient employment and development an ever increasing mystery; and those terms which are pre-eminently comprehensive, such as truth,

---

* C. P. CRANCH.

harmony, wisdom, must proportionably surpass other terms in their acquired mysteriousness, or power of taking by surprise the inexperienced thinker. Before proceeding to a consideration of the connection between Bible-worship and Pantheism, it may be well to contemplate some of the ideal relations of the word, Wisdom.

Human wisdom, being the extent to which men may have progressed in the knowledge of truth, is evidently a phrase of variable meaning. Wisdom, as an object of attainment, is thus distinguished from itself as a subject of aspiration. In other words, it is practically divisible into the smaller province which is already attained, and therefore now demonstrable, and into the larger province which is yet attainable, and therefore as yet mystical; and the line of demarkation must generally, if not always, lie differently in different minds, or in the same mind at different times. The neglect of this observation is a frequent source of confusion and misunderstanding, in the adoption and application of important rules of conduct.

To him who is indeed enough of a Christian to be able to say on all occasions, " I am nothing, Christ is all," there is no longer any distinction between the light of nature and the light of grace. The " Wisdom" of which King Solomon writes in Proverbs (chap. viii.) strikingly corresponds with the " Word" of the Evangelist John, and evidently means nothing less than the Supernatural Power which is ever controllingly present in nature, and which is also nearer to the souls which submit to its internal government than anything else can be, or than they are to one another. The Evil Spirit, the only evil which may lawfully, rationally, or efficiently be resisted, having fled from the manifestation of the Divine Power which becomes theirs by faith, all experience becomes to them a channel of divine revelation, and in all they are alike secure from the danger of mistaking the channel for the stream. That which is thus wholly true of the perfect Christian, would evidently be proportionably true of imper-

fect Christians of every degree, if they could be preserve(
from all exclusive or excessive attachment to particular mode:
of revelation.

So far, however, as any professor of Christianity shall fal
short of that perfect and immediate dependence upon th(
Divine Fountain which alone can secure an impartial indif
ference to the means of grace, his faltering self-denial canno
so overcome the prejudices of education, nor his partial en
lightenment so ignore the limitations of nature, but that som(
one science, record, or system, will be preponderatingly a rul(
of faith and revelation to him.   The abstract and comprehen
sive rule of the spiritual cross, although it will prevent hi:
resting in anything which is mere attainment to himself, can
not at once place him beyond a dependence upon that whicl
may be mere attainment to others; which dependence ma:
accordingly to them be indistinguishable from idolatry.   Thu:
it happens that the vanguard of civilization in our age i:
largely composed of more or less exclusive votaries of Biblica
and of Natural Science, who may be typified on the one han(
by those who term the Scriptures, the Word of God, and o:
the other by those who, because they are at a loss to distin
guish between the Creator and the created universe, are calle(
Pantheists.   Tradition is thus seemingly at variance with in
tuition, and history with theory.   But as all parties continu(
earnestly the pursuit of intrinsic truth, all may doubtless es
cape the dangers of their diverse bigotries, realizing in the lif(
of the Resurrection, the omnipresence of Him by whom "al
things were made," and " in whom all things consist."

THE LIFE OF GRACE.

THE world's the table of a mixed repast,
Contrived with wisdom, as with bounty, vast;
      Where Christian men
Relax in converse o'er their diverse cares,
Thence parting to resume their proper shares
      Of work again.

Refreshment quickens every hand and heart
Its several toil with zeal renewed to start,
      As Prudence gives
The tempered taste, true tongue, and willing ear,
Which carry on the current of good cheer
      By which it lives.

Thus man depends on Prudence. On itself
Alone, hangs Prudence. Human wit and pelf,
      As simple tools,
This effluence of Deity employs
To their behoof, who heed in all their joys
      Its mystic rules.

Man's mission is not to avoid the world,
But the denouncings which on it are hurled,
      In that it dreams
An independence of its own to nurse,
And for the better reason puts the worse
      In all its schemes.

So while we shun not, let us stoop, to eat,
Without base homage, our appointed meat;
      Remembering
That life above the world, in which we strive,
If we in labor be indeed alive
      And prospering!

103

Right thoughtfully, and thankfully, may we
O'er outward blessings study to agree ;
    And gladly share,
Without the blinding eagerness of sloth,
For relaxation and refreshment both,
    Our daily fare !

Then shall both strength and taste be e'er renewed
For public or for private fruits of good ;
    And we the grace
Attain, to seek but in the Father's will*
The meat which can the fainting spirit fill,
    In every place.

* "My meat is to do the will of Him that sent me, and to finish his work."—JOHN iv. 34.

THE KING OF WORDS.

"The natural man receiveth not the things of the Spirit of God ; for they are foolishness unto him : neither can he know them, because they are spiritually discerned."—I COR. ii. 14.

SOCIAL life may be said to be made up of the continual alternation of expression and interpretation. Every human being is in a limited sphere a sovereign issuing decrees by deed and by word ; and also, with less limitation, a subject receiving the decrees of God and his fellow-man, and responsible for their just interpretation and faithful execution. So far as his execution is indeed faithful, his service becomes sovereignty, and his interpretation is merged into an enlarged expression. So far as he is faithless, his performance must be a suicide of experience, or that capricious living in mere pleasure, which is scripturally affirmed to be a living death, and whose only positive and abiding result is the torment of a vicious interpretation, or the consciousness of perverted powers and lost opportunities. The most wicked life may indeed be unintentionally and obviously useful ; but its utility is no more attributable to the agent, than the power of thought and consciousness can be attributed to a steam-engine. He will be negatively dead to the partial good of his action, as he is positively dead in the commingling evil.

Men are naturally materialists. However it may have been with the origination of the race, its multiplication is evidently a material phenomenon. At the outset of individual life, matter is the basis of experience with all, and must so continue until the more or less complete subjugation of death,

hell and the grave, and the accompanying miraculous accession of the dividual and regenerate life of the spirit.   No one,
therefore, by whom that happy transformation is unattained,
is at any time capable of fully interpreting either himself or
his circumstances.   Hence the wondering query with which
those words and works of men which most truly reflect the
universal simplicity of objective nature, are at first almost
universally greeted, "What do they mean?"   But the quality
of truthful simplicity by which alone they are capable of compelling attention, being not only unfathomable but inconceiv-
able to a sensual discernment, the superficial querist learns to
regard rather the disposition of the doer or speaker than the
matter of his expression, as a more familiar, though not truly
more fathomable, subject of interpretation, and the term
"meaning" loses much or all of its force in contributing to
that of the term "Motive."   The servility of the sensual
nature thus conspires with the dignity of the spiritual, to
assign a commanding value to this mysterious but indispensable word.   The eccentricities of temperament and of training fail to offend when a conciliating Motive is supposed to
be involved in the instantaneous and deep-seated action of the
will.

The word Motive is not only thus of larger social signifi-
cance than the words Meaning and Method, but it is in an
even greater degree paramount to another, the word Object,
with which it is nevertheless still more liable to be confounded.
In his unregenerate incompetency to appreciate the abstract
foundations of thought, man is prone to overlook both the
motive proper or affectional germ of his proceeding, and its
intelligence or method, in the concrete aim or so-called object
of action ; thus giving all the force of the term Motive to the
thing which is determined rather than to the determining
principle, and miserably ignoring all law except the pretended rule of fate or chance.   Whoever says "motive" when he
means "object," countenances the delusion.   The impulse,
the method and the object, may indeed be said to form a

practically inseparable trinity of integral activity; but in so far as theory governs practice, the members of every trinity must be at least distinguished theoretically. The disposing motion of the soul, which is the primary development of volition, must evidently be the leading or immediately causative principle of human activity, and as such alone strictly entitled to the name of Motive. Being theoretically distinguishable from the action of the will, it is theoretically but a viceroy of conduct: but as the ever-acting viceroy, practically indistinguishable from the determining royalty, it becomes the ultimate criterion in the estimate both of thought and of conduct, and therefore practically the King of the turbulent province of Language.

10

MOTIVES.

"I DWELL in the valley of Conscience, like all men,
    Invested on both sides by towering mountains.
Self-Knowledge, my dwelling I also may call, when
    I reach under ground the mysterious fountains.

"Mount Strength, or Mount Virtue, ascends on the right hand;
    Its fellow is named, either Action, or Station :—
This, lost to the view in clouds darker than night, and
    That, shining in all the fair hues of creation.

"Contentment and service are paramount duties :
    Where both are maintained there can be no transgression :
Lo ! here I continue, in sight of yon beauties,
    With cheerfulness ploughing my petty possession.

"Can more be commanded ?"—Yes, sluggard in spirit !
    Hast thou all forgotten the under-ground fountains ?
Thy shuffling devotion can never inherit
    The riches that robe the Delectable Mountains.

The flowers and fruits thus attracting thy vision
    Away from the grandeurs of primal existence,
Like them must indeed set at naught thy ambition,
    Except thou unite with the proffered assistance.

The under-ground fountains connect with the mountains:
    Sink deep through the covering soil of thy nature !
Each stratum of duty holds one of those fountains,
    Whose mystical motion shall warrant thy way sure.

Though every rude element rises to frustrate,
    The prover of miracles never shall cower :
The deeper the doctrine thy life shall illustrate,
    The higher thy virtue shall publish its power.

RIVAL CLUES.

"They, measuring themselves by themselves, and comparing themselves among themselves, are not wise."—2 COR. x. 12.

AMID all the disputes and debates of purblind humanity, there is one fact which may be always assumed as indisputable. While theoretical truth is ever almost as incomprehensible as it is immutable, practical truth, or demonstrable experience, is as mutable as it is real. It is at least obviously verified at last in the experience of all, that nothing is settled or stationary in the fashion of the world which " passeth away." The phrase " established order" in its application to human institutions, is evidently at the best but a pious fiction or necessary artifice of language. In conversation we can only deal with spiritual power or causation, as spiritual life is manifested in material phenomena and changes ; and all mutual intelligence respecting any truly established order of experience, must accordingly imply a spiritual communion maintained independently of the works and words in which it is embodied, and which are themselves the life of the superficial liver. Force and form, though in themselves inseparable, are contrasting, and too often conflicting elements of human experience. Force is as fundamental and permanent, as it is essentially indemonstrable. Form is as superficial and transient, as it is essentially manifest. Force is meaning : form is expression.

Human character is the combined result of selection and experience. At the option of the agent, it either floats and drifts recklessly with form, or it dives and swims intelligently with force. In its conversational aspect, however, even character is necessarily and wholly formal and mutable, and as such, is always, like other recognized phenomena, a proper subject of constant inquiry with those whose powers of abstraction may not qualify them for viewing it in its essence, and so for laboring, here as elsewhere, to extend rather than to define the boundaries of the demonstrable. The explorer of truth must therefore ever be prepared to encounter the inquiry, *Who is greatest?* since there are always those who are thus compelled to base their arguments on the authority of character. Although the comparison of attainments thus instituted must ultimately yield to him the tribute of increasing reputation, the disappointment at the loss of companionship on such occasions is poorly compensated by the consequence of becoming himself an authority, and would be a constant source of unhappiness to him, were not the whole creation an inexhaustible reservoir of divine refreshment, to which the lover of truth may ever resort for communion with truly kindred souls, in the power and presence of the all-sufficing Provider. The alienation where unintentional may be regarded as unavoidable. Although a seeming or formal loss, it must then be an actual or potential gain to all parties, since even the servile imitator may thereby learn that the inquiry, *What is true?* comprehends his own, and every subordinate clue of investigation, and is not comprehended by them. Practical incongeniality being, in this world of work, the very voice of fate, becomes thus the rule of rank ; and as the majesty of truth is imparted to the · independent servants of truth, the partisans of every rival clue are led to recognize in their own shortcomings the delusions of all worldly or finite attainment, and are constrained increasingly to respect, if not to realize, the all-embracing claims of religion—the " great mystery of godliness."

COMPARISON.

To compare is to show we suspect :
　　To suspect is to publish our blindness :
To be blind, where we ought to detect,
　　Is brute-dullness or willful unkindness.

For the Spirit of Unity gives
　　In true kindness our social foundation,
As each tenant compatibly lives
　　With the plan of our joint habitation.*

As experience ever reveals
　　His own powers and objects in others,
He who knows his own tenement, feels
　　Its accordance, so far, with his brother's.

Thus the method is open to all
　　To employ that direct intuition,
By whose guidance man never can fall
　　Into dangerous trust or suspicion.

But the concert of spirit with form
　　Is a riddle which mocks the unwary,
So that prejudice takes them by storm
　　When the forms of propriety vary.

For the Spirit is that which gives life,
　　While the form is a fugitive seeming,
As is proved in that war to the knife
　　Which distinguishes seeing from dreaming.

And the mushroom assurance of those
　　By whom shells are devoured as kernels,
Through their love of comparison grows
　　From the compost of cast-off externals.

* " Ye also are builded together for an habitation of God through the Spirit."—Eph. ii. 22.

FAITH AS A GIFT.

"It is not reason that we should leave the Word* of God, and serve tables."—Acts vi. 2.

"If we were forced to form conceptions about a Son of God, or Son of Man, there would be a perpetual strife of intellects; there could be no consent; each man must think differently from his neighbor,—must try to establish his own thoughts against his neighbor's. If He is revealed to us as the ground of our intellects,—the Creative Word of God from whom they derive their light,—as the Centre of our fellowship, the only-begotten Son of God in whom we are made the sons of God; the weary effort is over: our thoughts may travel to the ends of the earth, but here is their home: apart from Him men have infinite disagreements; in Him they have peace."

F. D. Maurice.

IT may be regarded as a testimony against the assumption of a false independence, or a rash reliance upon any apparent originality of the individual human understanding, that we are scripturally taught that "faith comes by hearing." It may equally be regarded as a testimony against a false dependence upon the understandings of our fellow-men, that it is added, "and hearing by the word† of God." As there is such a thing as holding the truth in unrighteousness,‡ it is evident that the words of God may become the words of designing men, who would abuse the confidence of their fellows by applying them to occasions which do violence to their spiritual meaning. Words are many, because notions or ideas are many, as the constituent elements and circumstances of life in which they both originate are many. The Word of Truth is one, and is the Begetter of just notions, and may be said to

* Λόγος, the Word speaking. † 'Ρῆμα, the word spoken. ‡ Rom. i. 18.

112

be also the Namer of them, according to the circumstances of their birth. Its creations may thus become the objects of memory, and the means of imposture ; but It alone is the object of true faith, and the unchanging and ever new meaning of all expressions, old or new, which are uttered in the Divine authority, light and guidance, which can alone ensure a just appreciation of the circumstances. It is important to bear carefully in mind this necessarily vague distinction of spiritual from merely intellectual truth, however paradoxical or however obvious it may be to different classes of thinkers, in order to avoid the natural tendency, both to deceive ourselves by exaggerating the stability of our notions, and to impose upon others by assuming their universality.

The perspicuous, though elaborate, " Apology " of Robert Barclay, is a rich reservoir of suggestion upon the objects, and consequently upon the natures, of the true and the false faith. There appears to be a danger in our day, that men shall deny the possibility of a false faith. Let such, if such there be, consider that it cannot be more absurd to speak of a false faith, than of a false god, or of a false church, as a thing to which all are in danger of becoming victims if they do not diligently guard their own hearts !

The " Apology " is remarkable as being perhaps the first doctrinal treatise of permanent value in the world, which endorses the originally scholastic, but now inevitable, distinction between the subjective and objective aspects of experience. The ordinary use of these terms in the science of Grammar, sufficiently defines them. " Subjective " means of the originator or of the agent; " Objective," of the end, or of the material used. All practice implies the combination of the two aspects ; and faith, as the essential principle of intelligent practice, may be said to imply the concentration of each. There must be pre-eminently a combination of the subjective and the objective aspects of experience, in the deep, but fundamental phenomenon of pure faith.

Previously to the formal discrimination of these opposite,

though consistent aspects of faith, it is obvious that the thinker who was regarding it from one point of view, would be
apt to speak of the opposite aspect as a mere quality of faith,
rather than the thing itself.   While we read of faith as being
in itself "a substance," we also read, on the one hand, of the
"obedience of faith," which is evidently its essential condition ; and on the other, of the "assurance of faith," which is
its most apparent result and indication, and which accordingly in a superficial view may be mistaken for the substance.
In this comparatively superficial and secondary sense, it is
undeniable that faith is a gift ; and a gift of such importance
as to account for its being scripturally enumerated as such
among the other graces of the Spirit.   But that it is not to be
recognized as a part of the free and universal grace which
has been so dearly purchased for us in advance of our own
co-operation, is plainly intimated by a precise interpretation
of Eph. ii. 8 ("it is the gift of God"), and by Heb. iv. 2
("the word preached did not profit them, not being mixed
with faith in them that heard it").   The slightest acquaintance with the Greek language suffices to show that in the
former of these texts, it is the salvation, and not the faith,
which is called "the gift."   In an argumentative exhorta-
tion, does not this prompt reiteration of the view of the divine
mercy imply that, by the mention of faith, the apostle was
conscious of having interposed the view of something which
must be "of ourselves?"   In the latter text, faith is evidently
referred to exclusively in the aspect of obedience or submission.

Some extracts from the concluding section of Barclay's
defence of the second Proposition of his "Apology," upon
the subject of Revelation, may perhaps here serve to illustrate
"the form of sound words" which, as discovered, we are enjoined to maintain through all the advances of faith.

"To make an end, I shall add one argument to prove, that
this inward, immediate, objective revelation, which we have
pleaded for all along, is the only sure, certain and unmov-

able foundation of all Christian faith ; which argument, when well weighed, I hope will have weight with all sorts of Christians ; and it is this :

" That which all professors of Christianity, of what kind soever, are forced ultimately to recur unto when pressed to the last ; and that for and because of which all other foundations are recommended, and accounted worthy to be believed, and without which they are granted to be of no weight at all, must needs be the only most true, certain, and unmovable foundation of all Christian faith.

" But inward, immediate objective revelation by the Spirit, is that which all professors of Christianity are forced ultimately to recur unto, etc.

" First, as to the *Papists*, they place their foundation in the judgment of the *Church* and *tradition*. If we press them to say, Why they believe as the *Church* doth ? their answer is, *Because the Church is always led by the infallible Spirit.* So here *the leading of the Spirit* is the utmost foundation. Again, if we ask them, Why we ought to trust *tradition?* they answer, *Because these traditions were delivered unto us by the doctors and fathers of the Church ; which doctors and fathers, by the revelation of the Holy Ghost, commanded the Church to observe them.* Here again all ends in the revelation of the Spirit.

" As for the *Protestants* and *Socinians*, both which acknowledge the *Scriptures* to be the foundation and rule of their faith ; the one as subjectively influenced by the Spirit of God to use them, the other as managing them with and by their own reason ; ask both, or either of them, Why they trust in the *Scriptures*, and take them to be their rule ? their answer is, *Because we have in them the mind of God delivered unto us by those to whom these things were inwardly, immediately, and objectively revealed by the Spirit of God ;* and not because this or that man wrote them, but because the *Spirit of God* dictated them.

" Therefore, this inward, immediate, objective revelation by the Spirit, is the only sure, certain, and unmovable foundation of all Christian faith.

"It is strange that men should render [*i. e.*, account and report] that so uncertain and dangerous to follow, upon which alone the certain ground and foundation of their own faith is built; or that they should shut themselves out from that holy fellowship with God, which is only enjoyed in the Spirit, in which we are commanded both to walk and to live.

"Wait then for this in the small revelation of that pure light which first reveals things more known; and as thou becomest fitted for it, thou shalt receive more and more, and by a living experience easily refute their ignorance who ask, How dost thou know that thou art actuated by the Spirit of God? Which will appear to thee a question no less ridiculous than to ask one whose eyes are open, How he knows the sun shines at noonday? And though this be the surest and certainest way to answer all objections; yet by what is above written it may appear, that the mouths of all such opposers as deny this doctrine may be shut, by unquestionable and unanswerable reasons."

FORM.

MAKE not too light of form! All faith
    Implies a system. First,
    'Tis true, the germ must burst
Its shell; but as it grows it saith:

" A grain of living seed am I:
    I drop my rigid shell
    Which served my need so well,
And to my old existence die.

" And still I live. I do not scorn
    That shape, once so secure;
    But still its marks endure,
While my free strength is upward borne.

" I know not how I live and grow,
    Except that with my eye
    I love the light, and die
To naught through which my life can flow.

" New forms come o'er me: their design
    I act, but may not search.
    And yet in nature's church
Some humble consequence is mine.

" They come and go: but through them all
    I am myself, and still
    Reflect that Sovereign Will
To which the universe is thrall."

So let thy life its worship show!
    Do homage to his might;
    Eye lovingly his light;
Nor scorn through fleeting forms to grow!

THE KNOWLEDGE OF GOOD AND EVIL.

"Keep thy heart with all diligence; for out of it are the issues of life."—
PROV. iv. 23.

BY the law of Comparison which must govern our estimate
of all external things so far as they may be imaginarily,
either willingly or unwillingly, abstracted from their internal
relations, the demonstrable objects of knowledge are divided
into things general and things particular. Only by this law
is there any force in the contrasted terms Whole and Part, or
Summary and Detail; and since comparison itself is a process rather than a fact, even the distinction thus imparted
becomes as fugitive in its realization, as it was faulty in its
foundation. The process itself therefore becomes more worthy
of our attention, than the objects of it; and this we at once
find to be appreciable in two aspects, according to the direction in which the intelligent subject may be said to move in
its performance. So far as his course of investigation may
be one of mere dissipation, his knowledge of generals will
be lost in that of particulars, and he may be less justly said ac-
tively to analyze, than passively to decompose. So far as his
course may be one of labor and aspiration, his analysis will
be but the prelude to a synthesis of re-composition, or new
composition, and he will thus ascend from the knowledge of
particulars to that of generals.

Whatever we may think of the cause, the fact is a glaring
one, that it is only through analysis that we rise to synthesis.
Every man naturally tends to rely upon some partial phase
of truth which is his ideal of Deity, if not the "god of his

118

idolatry," so long as his nature remains undeveloped into the perfect catholicity of pure love. Appetite; intellect; the moral wealth or credit which consists in the possession of reputation; the more glaringly material blessings which are in like manner represented by money; even a genuine human fellowship so far as it can be maintained out of a conscious subordination to the Divine Power and impersonal principles of truth, are all to be classed among external things, and are mere surfaces and semblances of substantial good. They are alike dangerous abstractions, although temporarily necessary to stay the longings of our fragmentary nature for the one undeceitful and eternal concrete. At best they are but finite and fugitive forms of the One Infinite and Immutable Force. It is necessary for us to recognize them as practical powers; but it is possible to elevate them from the service of guides to the station of idols, and to sacrifice to them our hope of perfect good, instead of devoting them continually upon the altar of truth, as the price and proof of progress in the knowledge of God.

By the intellect, or mind, the truth is known in its details. Only by faith and hope can it be approached in its integrity, and only by love can it be finally and perfectly realized. The intellect is the storehouse of knowledge, but the heart is its living source, because it is the seat of spiritual belief. The trust in intellect may therefore be called a false faith, as opening a door for the delusions of self and Satan. " In vain the net is spread in the sight of any bird." It is only as we practically ignore the dependence of head-work upon heart-work, that the Power of evil can profit by our limitations, and make us pervert to our loss the lessons of experience by which we might otherwise " go on to perfection."

The head may be termed the seat of form, as the heart is that of force. Accordingly, since knowledge is the command of mere forms, while realization includes also that of forces, the knowledge of good and evil may evidently be the occasion, although it cannot be the cause, of disobedience to the

11

law written or spoken in the heart.   The cause must evidently be a want of faith in the unseen, and a consequent dependence upon the deceitful forms of knowledge.   Forsaking the true inspiration, man is at the mercy of a false inspiration which can act upon him only by an appeal to some sort of precedent. Rejecting the privilege of co-operating with an ever present and almighty Creator, he then shuts himself in the tomb of past experiences.   His work of synthesis may be but begun, when he shall forsake it in a voluntary blindness, and descend into that of a fruitless analysis.   Let him beware of so realizing the decomposition of corruption!

Blessed indeed and for ever be the Eternal Father of Spirits for the advent of the Second Adam, who through all dangers and temptations, is " mighty to save and able to deliver all them that come unto God by Him!"

IMMORTALITY.

SOME dreaming souls there are in this dim world,
  Who care not to discern the Why and How
That Will appears, whose power of old unfurled,
  And still expands, the streaming I and Now.

To them creation is a lie ; and fate
  The mirror of their life, which represents
Confusion and distress as the estate,
  And final grave, of all the elements.

Too torpid they the urgent signs to heed
  Of that primeval One, whose skill supreme
Called forth from naught, or from Himself decreed,
  The scenes which decorate their willful dream.

Alike unknown to them the supplement
  To that prime miracle ;—how life prevails
O'er death, by healing grace, with force not spent,
  But fed, in graver or more trifling ails.

Thus never come, but always going, life
  To them, it seems, suggests no mystery.
The I and Now with them are so at strife,
  The Why and How they cannot wish to see.

So may we know the central Source of light,
  So may its flood our finite measures fill,
That the creative and redemptive Might
  May prove in every pass our treasure still !

Then fate to us can offer no dismay :
  The star that brightly sets is never gone ;
But through the spheral sky of faith, with ray
  Unfaltering moves, and shines for ever on.

SINCERITY AND SENSIBILITY.

"The secret of the Lord is with them that fear Him."—Ps. xxv. 14.
"If any man will do his will, he shall know of the doctrine."—JOHN vii. 17.

ALTHOUGH there is no identity, there is certainly no incompatibility, between wisdom and knowledge. Their difference is indeed obvious to the reflecting observer, but it may perhaps here be appropriately remarked that wisdom is a state of the soul, while knowledge is a process of intercourse between the soul and outward things. Their relation to each other is the same as that which exists between physical health and physical performance. Accordingly, as knowledge, by the testimony of universal experience, is practically equivalent to physical power of every kind, wisdom is obviously, as the voice of inspiration anciently declared, "the principal thing," or that which is worthy to be pursued and cherished as the only permanent channel of every inferior blessing. Remembering that the relation of the internal to the external is that of cause to effect, we may describe the order of human experience by saying that performance is the surface of health, health the surface of knowledge, and knowledge the surface of sensibility or active wisdom. Cannot the state of wisdom be also viewed as a still more recondite process of some deeper and simpler element of being? Let us examine whether it be not itself a comparatively outward manifestation of secret sincerity of soul, and whether the convenient distinction between states and processes be not ever a merely relative one, whose line of division recedes before the penetration of the inquirer, as does that between the internal

122

and the external in every field of research. The investigation may seem to deal in insignificant refinements; but let us ever remember that in what may be called intellectual optics, as in the physical science, the same principles, which, when applied in one direction, may bring into view the most distant recesses of the field of vision, in the other may reveal the harmonious order by which the infinitely small co-operates with the infinitely vast. Let us explicitly inquire whether the wisdom which is passive as compared with practical knowledge, may not be regarded as active from a more internal point of view; and, if so, by what terms we shall designate the relatively passive and active, or internal and external results of our more advanced analysis.

As neither power nor consciousness, although to an evident extent under our own control, can be said to originate in our own volition, every human being may be said to be practically a compound of materials and susceptibilities. The secondary phenomena of power and consciousness being determined by the greater or less harmony of the human will with the Divine Will, even the human will, being thus at best but a power of choice between the solicitations of more potent influences, must practically rank with mere susceptibilities or capacities. As the link, however, between the agent and the impersonal power of his action, it is evidently the bond of unity to his whole life, so far as he may lead a consistent life. If, then, by this power of choice he shall devote himself to the service of the Omnipresent Spirit of Good, its inwardly and outwardly uniting influence must preserve him from the dividing influence of the adverse Spirit of Evil; and his life will exhibit the impress of sincerity to those who, by a like acquaintance with the source of sincerity, are qualified to appreciate its harmonious manifestations. Sincerity being thus, whether recognized or not, the pervading trait, not only of his manifest actions, but of all the peculiarities of character by which he may be distinguished from other agents, and which only may strictly be called his individual traits, becomes evi-

11 *

dently with all such the individual channel or measure of power, and the basis of true, manly consciousness.

Power being thus inseparable from consciousness in spiritual experience, the two must increase or decrease together. As sincerity is another name for individual power, so is sensibility for individual consciousness. The sphere of perception must clearly rise with that of action, as the course of attainment successively reduces the objects of our short-sighted, although spiritual, aspirations, to the rank of animal qualifications, so that the capacity of appreciation will ever continue to be a measure of the capacity of performance. In other words sensibility will ever keep pace with sincerity, and be the active component of wisdom, so far as it may be necessary to distinguish wisdom from knowledge, and the conscious royal and priestly man, from the superficial and servile human machine. We recognize morality as a living power, or the true handmaid of religion, when we proclaim, in the language of a venerable teacher, * that sincerity is its " touchstone."

* DANIEL B. SMITH. of Philadelphia.

SCEPTRES.

WHAT sceptre will the model monarch wield,
At which the demon Anarchy shall yield
His horrid waste, and perish on the field?

The sword affrights : but how, if FEAR be lord
Shall Anarchy not often be restored
As blind Contention shall her aid afford?

Gold weighs and shines : right strong 'twould seem is GOLD.
But how shall stand a thousand, so controlled,
Before one will which never has been sold?

Friendship may smile ; and LOVE is surely strong,
Were smiles but love, the fiend could live not long,
But love avowed, means license, to the throng.

To sway the throng the sceptre must be twined.
Three rigid cords in one must be combined,
Ere stands the rule which shall not be resigned.

Take purity, which shuns diverting cares ;
Patience, to which contempt its secret bares ;
And vigilance, which no occasion spares.

Where LOVE shall move embodied in these three ;
Hiding and hidden, where they all agree ;
There shall be waved the wand of Majesty.

AFFECTATION AND EMULATION.

APPEARANCES are manifold and mysterious: realities are few and simple. Substantial good and essential evil, therefore, however readily distinguished by those whose faculties, in the words of the Apostle, are "exercised by reason of use," are sadly confounded by those who have not learned to look beneath appearances. None but those who understand the divine command to "judge not according to the appearance," need attempt to obey the subsequent apostolic precept, "abstain from all appearance of evil," since it is evident, on the one hand, that they alone can know what a true appearance of evil is; and on the other, that any, in shunning a false appearance of it, must be shunning a real good.

Let it be remembered then, that appearances are to be studied, and cultivated or suppressed, only so far as they are incidental to realities, and not as they may depend on the fallible notions of our fellow-men, which they alone, of mortals, can rectify. Thus we may hope to avoid the vice of affectation, and to grow in consistency by the practice of a true independence.

As affectation is the frequent foible of advanced years, so emulation is the besetting danger of the season of youth; for it also may be said to have its source in an undue regard for mere appearances. Both evils may exist in varying degrees, although either of course becomes generally conspicuous only when unusually intense. They differ in the circumstance that

while affectation becomes conspicuous only through extraordinary ignorance of the subject which is the occasion of it,
emulation is most obvious when it is joined with extraordinary
knowledge. When not thus joined, emulation often appears
as a desire rather to equal those who may be in advance
of us, than to surpass those who are in the same stage of
progress, and thus becomes more indistinguishable from a
laudable love of approbation. In both cases, however, the
stimulus of mere emulation is distinguishable, to a disinter-
ested observer, from that of the pure love of truth and good
report, by the different effects of success and failure upon the
different aspirants. Where emulation is the motive, success
will be followed by a temporary relaxation of zeal, the apparent earnestness of the worker giving place to a real levity
of manner, because the motive itself fails, and no stream can
flow faster or higher than its source. To the sincere lover of
truth, on the other hand, present success is valuable chiefly
as an opening for future progress in truth, and accordingly
stimulates him at once, though perhaps unconsciously, to renewed exertion. For the same reasons the occasional failure
which in the one case brings manifest pain and mortification,
is encountered in the other without disappointment, and may
even afford apparent encouragement through the new suggestions which it is always able to supply.

The intelligent Christian needs but little argument to re-
mind him, that an escape from both affectation and emulation
is to be found only in the earnestness of purpose, which the
religion of the Cross only can supply to those in whose experience there is any remaining antagonism between realities
and appearances. In individual as in social life, it alone is
the reconciling agency, through which the only Saviour of
men " slays the enmity" of the discordant elements, " making
in Himself of twain one new man, so making peace."

I

BUCKRAM.

THE good and ill combine in every breast,
   Like sheep and goats within the seeming church,
Or wheat and tares, confused and unconfessed
   Until the harvest-binders' rigid search.

But not the less may every human heart
   Which owns the Light that shines upon its sores,
And courts the heavenly breeze, and bears the smart
   By which its inward balm to health restores,—

Not less shall he who makes that Light his home,
   Each end from its beginning learn to see.
The day of judgment, thus already come,
   To its disclosures summons thee and me.

The mongrel traits in thy heart and in mine,
   Strange offspring of contending good and ill,
As thus discerned shall show their clear design,
   Nor fickle nature veil the constant will.

The charity which grafts the soul in God,
   And from such union all its increase knows,
Shall stand unmoved when earth and heaven shall nod,—
   The earth and heaven of willful works and shows.

The earnestness which breeds self-sacrifice,
   Of charity must largely be inspired,
Though oft appearing zealous more than wise,
   And safely gain the glorious goal desired.

But he who takes the stiffness for the strength,
   And imitates thereby the earnest man,
Shall lean upon a broken reed at length.
   Let thee and me our own foundation scan !

ASSURANCE, SENTIMENTAL AND PRACTICAL.

" He that doeth these things shall never be moved."—Ps. xv. 5.
" That ye may have somewhat to answer them which glory in appearance, and not in heart."—2 Cor. v. 12.

IT is so evidently disgraceful for man, as a being created in the image of God, to be living in a state of mental suspense, or in any sort of dependence on mere circumstances, that it is not to be wondered at, that the mere reputation of holy assurance, or settlement of soul and fixity of purpose, should often be a coveted prize with those who are ignorant of the reality. The true rule for distinguishing between a pretended assurance and a real one, thus becomes a matter of importance to the sincere inquirer and earnest worker, so far as he may be required in any way to respond to the pretensions or professions of his fellow-men.

Here as elsewhere general doctrine can be approached only by the way of particular experience, and enforced by an appeal to the same. There is a modest egotism and a cautious dogmatism which are less open to the insinuation of error than officious self-depreciation or ambitious argumentation ; and the most enthusiastic propagandism cannot substitute individual heart-work, nor communicate the vision in which alone heart is said to answer to heart, " as face to face " in outward reflection. (Prov. xxvii. 19.) " We preach," wrote the great apostle of doctrine, " not ourselves, but Christ Jesus the Lord ; and ourselves your servants for Jesus' sake" (2 Cor. iv. 5) : and again, ranking himself among the learners,

"Whereto we have already attained, let us walk by the same rule, let us mind the same thing." (Phil. iii. 16.)

Of the faith which may be had "to ourselves before God" as the same teacher elsewhere enjoins (Rom. xiv. 22), we of course cannot directly demonstrate the grounds, one to another. It is of those relations to man, which though similar to our relations to God, are subordinate thereto, or are involved in them, and so rather imply than involve those superior ties, it is of these alone that we can hope clearly to demonstrate the nature and operation to each other. The assurance that he has discharged his duty toward men, and is therefore free from any particular obligation to others resulting from previous trespass or neglect on his own part, is therefore the highest practical prerogative which may be claimed for the Christian freeman, or that by which he pre-eminently maintains his position and influence in the world of society.

This practical or social assurance may be said to consist in the habitual consciousness of self-sacrifice or devotion.* Devotion to man is a more distinct object of consciousness than devotion' to God, simply because we are more continually reminded of our past services to one another by the almost necessary imperfectness of their appreciation. The humble Christian is reminded of his past service to God, only by its abundant remuneration; and his appreciation of, or thankfulness for this, is often too far from being continual, so that his assurance God-ward may be less conscious, if not less real, than his assurance man-ward. As is set forth in the parable of the Unjust Steward, "the children of this world" may upon this point be more discerning respecting "the children of light," than they themselves are, "in their generation." The same weakness of an immature faith is clearly intimated in the oft-quoted interrogatory, "If a man love not his brother whom he hath seen, how can he love God, whom he hath not seen ?"† and may well account for the greater attainability and more frequent appearance of the lower order of assurance,

---

* See p. 131, margin. † I JOHN iv 20.

among those who are as yet only on the way to the state of the spiritual man, who "judgeth all things."

We may infer then that the strongest assignable evidence of that higher assurance God-ward is to be found in this lower assurance man-ward, which, with its naturally attendant graces of accessibility, geniality and frankness, is at once essential and sufficient for the preservation of merely social position. It may be regarded, to borrow a scriptural simile, as the candle-stick of the Gospel candle, whether the flame of individual aspiration may as yet be confined to the form of confession and prayer, or whether it may have expanded into that of praise and boasting in God alone. Where this principle is justly appreciated, there can be little or no danger of a mere general doctrinal profession being allowed to supersede that specific personal confession, which " is made unto salvation" as the fruit of repentance and the pledge of amendment.

✱✱ [*Note to 2d Edition : see reference from p. 130.*]

Let not an erratic zeal or a false humility carp at this sentiment as being self-conceited. There can be no practical Christianity without a more or less thorough "self-sacrifice and devotion;" nor any real self-sacrifice and devotion, without ensuing consciousness of the same, and the ability and occasional duty to assert it. Hence that apostolic paradox, already cited, " We preach not ourselves, but . . . ourselves, etc."

12

TONE.

THE crown of virtue is endurance ;—
  That time, and time's o'erturnings,
May not subdue her mild assurance,
  Or dissipate her earnings.

Her gathered strength, and current favor
  Rare tact, and common chattel,
Maintain the ranks which shall not waver
  Through life's unceasing battle.

" But by what magic, or what training,
  Rules she her matchless legions,
Herself and them so well sustaining
  Through dark and hostile regions ?"

Lo ! virtue is the Sun of heaven,
  Which lays each night-born terror,
And quickens with transforming leaven
  The very mists of error !

" Yes ! such is virtue in her pureness.
  But how can mortals reach her,
Whose thinking sullies all their sureness,
  Or other erring teacher ?"

Inconstant heart ! forsake thy doubting !
  The sun thou knowest by vision,
Doth not salute thy ear with shouting
  To deepen thy decision.

Lift watchfully to virtue's shinings
  The worship of thy spirit,
And thou shalt yet with her refinings
  Her energies inherit !

RULES OF RATIONAL CONVERSATION.

"To him that ordereth his conversation aright will I show the salvation of God."—Ps. l. 23.
"By thy words thou shalt be justified, and by thy words thou shalt be condemned."—MATT. xii. 37.

I. UNIVERSAL, OR ABSOLUTE.

A. LET there be but one subject whose nature and connections are to be examined and discussed at one time.

II. CONDITIONAL, OR RELATIVE.

B. Let the subject thus immediately under consideration be always, if possible, a thing, act or principle, and not a person or character.

C. Where any one, from incapacity or heedlessness, finds it more easy to judge an agent as evil or as good, than to define the evil or the good of his action or language, and proceeds to the expression of such judgment, let him promptly and modestly, if invited, confess the motive of zeal or benevolence which actuated him : but, if he shall find upon reflection that he could honestly and charitably have judged the performance rather than the performer, or wholly have suppressed his judgment, let him not attempt any such justification ; but on the contrary, if permitted, acknowledge and condemn the transgression of his lips, briefly, but unreservedly.

General Remarks. There is something which is almost contradictory in the very mention of an Universal Rule; since by a Rule we mean nothing less than an intelligible principle or clue which may lead us through a labyrinth of unknown because ever multiplying circumstances. The verbal demonstration of any intelligible principle to be universally applicable to circumstances which are in any sense unknown, is indeed a hopeless task. The epithet Universal is therefore here of importance, not as one which is safe from the chance of misconception, but merely as one which is necessary to denote the difference which appears by a comparison of the first rule with the two others. If either of the three is of any value, it is because there is a spirit in it which underlies and gives life to its letter. The spirit of the first rule may be called universal, because it consists essentially in the simple reverence for truth, as truth. That rule implies that there is no fact or circumstance which is so trivial in itself or in its actual relations, that it is not worthy of the most protracted attention which we are capable of bestowing upon it ; and that our inability to trace its influence to an indefinite extent in every direction, is solely owing to our want of such a microscopic acuteness and such a telescopic range of intellectual vision, as the just appreciation of nature requires. Facts which might otherwise be regarded as isolated and unimportant, are thus by a sort of natural faith presumed, apart from the evidence of perception, to be essential constituents in one great scheme of universal truth, even before this scheme may be distinctly realized as a beneficent instrumentality, by which the God of nature and of grace is ever working out his own glory and the happiness of his obedient children. This rule may therefore be said to be based on an acknowledgment of that " first and great commandment" of love to God, as the others may upon that of " the second," or love to our fellow-man. When the one shall indeed become in every sense universal, the others will doubtless become superfluous, and therefore obsolete ; as is certified by the strong public sentiment which already stamps personalities as being irrelevant in all kinds of useful discussion. Since, therefore, with the increased prevalence of the rule which has been styled Universal, those which have been styled Conditional must become still more exceptional, these designations may perhaps be seen so to illustrate one another, as to show that the distinction must be recognized as an experimental fact.

Particular Remarks. (*A.*) Of course there are difficulties in adopting this rule, not only from the diversity of views and suggestions which may arise in the minds of different persons in the same company on the same occasion, but also on account of the hesitancy which any individual may feel in selecting as most worthy of remark, from among the throng of suggestions which may arise in his own mind, that which is most naturally or closely and evidently connected with the particular matter which may be at the moment under consideration. Both of these circumstances obviously tend to prevent the co-operation of thought and feeling in the development of intellectual or spiritual fruit, and to make our spoken converse an unnatural and unavailable medley of disunited and undigested details. These difficulties, however, it should be observed, may be said to be the very occasion for our requiring any rules at all on the subject, as being the main obstacles which occur in this field of operation, to the maintenance of that divine and diffusive harmony which is both the surest means and the worthiest end of all social aspirations. The rule therefore will be plainly entitled to our respect, so long as it may appear to be the best means by which these obstacles are kept in view, for the sake of enabling us, so far as may be possible, to avoid them. The following of the letter may not ensure the fulfillment of the rule, but the faithful following of the spirit does ensure that fulfilling of the spirit, which most contributes to present success and best qualifies for future progress. To obtain the benefit of the rule, therefore, we have only to follow the spirit as expressed by the letter, so far as it may suggest to our minds any intelligible and feasible applications.

12 *

One obvious suggestion which thus becomes binding in this rule is, the right of every member of a social gathering to throw into the common stock of entertainment, such views or illustrations of the matter under their joint consideration as his own sense of duty may demand from him. This privilege results from the simple fact of an abstract equality which is to be presumed in the rights of all who may recognize one another as companions ; and, if cherished as a piece of duty, will of course not be exercised in violation of social order : that is, not until others of the company, such as there generally are, who may be presumed to be more fully qualified for judging or explaining the matter, shall have had the opportunity of anticipating his remarks.—Another such suggestion, which seems immediately to flow from this, is the right and duty of any one to recur to a previous subject of conversation upon which he may have been prevented from speaking through deference to this principle of social order, but without in the mean time finding himself relieved from the obligation of utterance, either through an anticipation by others of his intended meaning, or by their incidentally convincing him of the inaccuracy or irrelevancy of his view. It may be observed indeed that the progress of any conversation necessarily implies an apparent change of the immediate subject, whether this changeful appearance may consist in the desultory rehearsal of facts and fancies without regard to their inherent or presumed connection, or in the more thoughtful movement among the minor details which may relate to an engrossing central theme : and the return from a hasty diversion or remote illustration will therefore of course, necessitate a real or seeming change of subject which will be more or less abrupt in proportion as the previous departure has been abrupt and protracted. But, under the circumstances supposed, the speaker will evidently not be responsible for this irregularity, if he shall have been only careful to avail himself of the first fair opportunity for delivering his sentiment.

Another suggestion, which is furnished rather by the spirit

than by the letter of this rule, is, that where one topic of
conversation appears to be exhausted (which indeed must
ever be only an appearing), from the general absence of disposition or material for comment on the part of all who may
be together on the occasion, a new subject of remark may be
introduced by any individual under a deliberate conviction of
its inherent propriety, and with due reference to the principle
of priority already mentioned as a part of social order. In
providing for the preservation of harmonious conversation, it
is of course necessary that the supply of appropriate subject
matter shall not be interrupted, and the obtrusion of that
which is inappropriate therefore indirectly invited, by any of
our rules : and such results might evidently ensue from a tenacious regard for the mere letter of that now remarked upon.

(B.) The two principal and most obvious reasons for this
rule, perhaps are, First ; That it is always impossible for one
person to know from any appreciable appearances, the motives
of another in any action, since they depend mainly upon the
condition of his heart, which is apparent only to the Supreme
Judge of the world, and not upon his visible or other physical
circumstances, which only are known, and that but imperfectly
to his fellow-men : and Second ; That such knowledge, were
it possible, would be always irrelevant, inasmuch as our dealings with other men must be regulated by the extrinsic character or current value of their performances. It is worthy
of remark, however, that one's natural endowments and deficiencies, and even those intellectual attainments and peculiarities which are the results of the culture and the custom
which may each alike be styled a " second nature," are justly
distinguishable from those governing dispositions and impulses
which spring immediately from the recesses of the heart, and
which alone are truly characteristic of the person as a responsible being. The one class of facts may therefore be
regarded as legitimate materials for conversation and inquiry,
while the other must remain a sort of forbidden fruit which

we cannot reach if we would, and could not use if we could pluck it.

(C.) If the preceding rules may be regarded as intelligible and useful, this, in conclusion, may be found almost to explain itself. If, as has just been intimated, a mistaken opinion or an habitual prejudice does not necessarily imply a vice of the will, being rather the passive material or instrument, than the very power, of the determining motive, the formal breach of social order here contemplated may obviously admit of justi-' fication on this ground. And what can be more truly suggestive and profitable to all parties, than the frank and timely, and yet unobtrusive and unintentional revelation of one's own infirmities and extravagances which is thus induced? If, on the other hand, the formal transgression shall prove to have actually resulted from a present fault of unwatchfulness in the speaker, the formal error becomes obviously more or less of a willful one, and, as such, is a proper subject for repentance and condemnation on the part of the transgressor. A just appreciation of the two other rules which have now been considered, will therefore require him to give utterance to such condemnation; while a becoming sense of humiliation, seconded by the same formal injunctions, may well prevent him from presuming to entertain or edify his hearers, with a precise estimate of the error of his motive or the condition of his heart.

Application. The preceding remarks and rules are offered for the consideration of those only who regard society as one of their fields of individual service. They are based upon the assumption that the earnest man seeks for no recreation or repose except that which is incident to the divinely ordained diversification of duty. As in every more limited field of action it is observable that an attempted compromise between rival principles results chiefly in confusion, so, in the great arena of social life, be it called a field of labor or one of strife, we find the strongest confirmation of the principle. There can be no rivalry admitted here between our convictions of duty and our anticipations of pleasure as the laws of action, but one of the two must be wholly subordinated and rendered tributary to the other, if any purpose whatever is steadily pursued. To those who acquiesce in the constant supremacy of the law of duty, however imperfectly or indirectly it may be revealed, the business of all life becomes but a varied work and a varied worship ; and among such the work of society is a true co-ordination and consummation of that of individuals, so that the "fruits of the Spirit" declare themselves with all the emphasis of an united experience, in "glory to God in the highest, peace on earth, and good-will to men."

It must be particularly observed that the proposed rules of conversation prescribe no mode of settling the question of personal precedence, which they necessarily assume as a question ever pending, and the decision of which depends upon the relative weight of personal character. Silence upon such a subject may, however, be more expressive than speech, since it cannot be held up as a subject of sufficient importance either for thought or for speech, except in so far as the title to such authority is indisputably displayed in the outward demonstration, through the obedience of faith and the growth of refinement, of the abstract power and progressive order of universal truth. This effective obedience, so far as it shall prevail, will beget an unvarying harmony and a practical equality, in which it may be fitly said, that all will rule and all will serve. Even an established preponderance, which may not amount to an entire prevalence, of this perfect loyalty in any branch of society, will constitute the condition of corporate freedom in which the laws are the most obvious and the most honored rulers, under the immediate influences of Heavenly Love ; for this established recognition of abstract principles of right which are universally appreciable, will become then a court of appeal by which all the breaches of social harmony may be both promptly and finally decided upon. As the recognized principles are in very deed the offspring of truth, they will bear witness to their parentage, by being few, simple, mutually illustrative, and mutually confirmative. Thus will they be open to the apprehension and application of all, being ever ready to aid the lover of truth in advancing the glory of the God of truth, by stifling the germs of slothful confusion, by exposing the pretensions of spurious dignity, and by silencing the clamor of hasty conceit.

LAW.

"By what constraint shall we invoke thee,
    Thou who withholdest fools from error?
What happy summons first awoke thee,
    And bade thee spread thy wholesome terror?

"Oh, rouse thee from thy lair of mystery,
    And make the world a home of gladness!
Let not the page of human history
    Be evermore a roll of sadness!"*

—Know, mortals! I am but a phantom.
    Look not to me for beds of roses!
My rule were a chaotic random,
    Had not each utterance its Moses.

My origin is aye among you:
    Not mainly from the might of princes,
Nor from the strains your seers have sung you,
    Your law salutes you, and convinces.

'Tis not the ballot of the voter:
    'Tis not the dogma of the student:
Than all by far an abler motor
    Is the example of the prudent.

One Ruler governs all your nations:
    His secret is with those that fear Him,
Who welcome all his dispensations,
    And live in firm allegiance near Him.

Like them rule ye each erring neighbor,
    Unwillingly, if not in blindness!
Spread with your hands the law of labor!
    Drop from your lips the law of kindness!

* " And lo! a roll of a book . . . And there was written therein lamentations, and mourning and woe."—Ezek. ii. 9, 10.

UNANIMOUS SUFFRAGE.

"Let me fall now into the hand of the Lord . . . but let me not fall into the hand of man."—I CHRON. xxi. 13.

"Let the potsherd strive with the potsherds of the earth."—ISA. xlv. 9.

"If two of you shall agree on earth as touching anything that they shall ask, it shall be done for them of my Father which is in heaven."—MATT. xviii. 19.

FOR thousands of years the Sword has been the idol of nations, the "forlorn hope" of righteous rulers, and the *ultima ratio*, the "last argument" of bewildered lawgivers. Within a few centuries a mighty competitor for its influence has been revealed to the world, in the outspoken claim of Majorities. The two modes of appeal are practically alike in so far as numbers may determine their decision, and also in so far as this more accidental indication may be overborne by the superior prowess, physically or intellectually, of superior men. But the voice of majorities is doubtless upon the whole the preferable rule, inasmuch as it is evidently based more upon permanent principles, and less upon passing phenomena. As regards eternal destiny all men are certainly born potentially " free" and actually "equal," the Universal Father being " no respecter of persons ;" and with nations, as with individuals, the most stable policy must clearly be that which subordinates the physical life to the spiritual. The recognized claim of majorities, being based upon the presumption of equality, is evidently an advance in the right direction, or toward the standard of spiritual perfection.

In this imperfect world, however, there is always some

danger of our carrying our ideal presumptions of perfection into practical extravagance. So long as either the sword or the ballot-box shall be to any extent necessary as an instrument of decision, it is evident that there must be some who are more fit to be governed than to govern, and who are therefore examples of a practical inequality. Apart from the consideration that by insisting upon the participation of such in the ceremonials of sovereignty we should weakly exaggerate the abstraction of equality and disparage that of freedom, it is note-worthy that we should thus inferentially ignore the doctrine, that man's first business in time is rather to serve than to rule. We should even practically impede the work of those who are indeed the public servants, since either the incompetent fighter or the incompetent voter must still farther impair his individual and social efficiency by his misplaced action.

The subordination of might to right is still to be the lesson of history. A healthy development of public opinion will yet, it may be hoped, supplant and substitute both sword and ballot as the swift terror to evil doers, and the sufficient praise to them that do well.* "Be of one mind," is the command which may be called the corner-stone of Christian government. To be of at least two minds, may be said to be an essential requirement of our now prevailing political systems. The once mysterious relations of Jew and Gentile may be regarded as typical of the isolating and conflicting interests of the fallen nature in every age. The holy "Captain of Salvation" lived, and died, and rose again, "that he might reconcile both unto God in one body by the cross, having slain the enmity thereby." The true soldier of the cross will always vote in practical influence; and he will never vote in vain, because, instead of feeding the external evil by a direct opposition, he will starve it, to the extent of his ability, by crucifying the internal evil. The measurement of might, either by arms or by numbers, cannot be the rule of right to one who

---

* ROM. xiii. 3; 1 PET. ii. 14.

K

holds that the government of heaven, though not indeed of the world, is ever in the world, as well as above the world. Neither contests nor confederations based upon mere worldly policy, can result in anything better than Babel-confusion, that being ever but a merely formal, if not a counterfeit zeal or unanimity, which is not immediately and individually derived from faith in the Divine Power, or from a resulting insight into the Divine Will.

POLITICS.

Some people live in a world of their own;
Some live in their surroundings;
And some, I ween, hold a worthier throne
With no provincial boundings.

To all their life is a spending of force,
For objects whole or hollow;
In all, the outlay expresses some source
From which such fruits may follow.

The throne that rules the unbroken extent
Of human works and pleasures,
From large resources its prowess will vent
In many ways and measures.

The scattered thrones of sectarian name
And wasting emulation,
With sudden impact and perishing fame
Betray their slight foundation.

" We stand united, divided we fall,"
The old, familiar presage,
Still hints its terrible warning to all,
And spirit-stirring message.

But let us join on a tenable ground,
Not in an empty seeming,
Standing from every constriction unbound
Which tells of selfish scheming.

Then private duty may furnish the force,
In harmony divided,
By whose advance in its gathering course
Both Church and State are guided.

THE LAST HERESY.

"Certainly there be those that delight in giddiness, and account it a bond-age to fix a belief."—BACON.

NEITHER orthodoxy nor heresy is anything, if it be not practical. Truth is the law as well as the lawful object of life, and doctrine is valuable only as the reflection of truth. Short of that universality of truth which is the ultimate test of practical orthodoxy, and in which all mysteries, distinctions and peculiarities are either eradicated or harmonized, all doctrine must have its subjective shortcoming, which can only await the development of events to become, and to be manifested as, practical heresy. While the subjective wisdom of one generation after another becomes incorporated in objective knowledge, the essential condition and congenital tendencies of human nature remain unchanged. The mysterious progress of partial doctrine toward universal truth is undoubtedly a collective as well as an individual work; but the responsibilities of individuals increase therein with their increasing advantages. "The light," said that genuine seer and faithful standard-bearer of gospel-truth, Isaac Pennington, "shineth more and more toward the perfect day; and it is not the owning of the light as it shone in the foregoing ages which will now commend any man to God, but the owning and subjecting to the light of the present age." The pertinacious profession of the light as it shone in the last age, may be the subtlest form of practical heresy.

It must be painfully evident to all who are indeed concerned to "stand in the ways and ask for the old paths" in order

146

that they may " see" their essential features, and truly " walk
therein," * that the great adversary of souls has in our day re-
sorted to what may be regarded as his last and most dangerous stratagem. By inducing a theoretical denial or actual
forgetfulness of his own existence, he is making men blind,
in their hour of outward security, to the essential nature of
evil, removing as it were the oldest and most serviceable way-
marks, and plausibly insinuating that human life is a diversified culture rather than a battle of doubtful issue, or that,
in the language of a current proverb, " all roads lead to the
Great City." If each of his victims will only contribute something to the recognition of this culminating heresy, he doubtless cares little how inconsistently orthodox they may be in
other respects.

The religion of Christ is the religion of the charity which
" thinketh no evil" of its neighbor. Christian charity, by remembering the infirmity of nature, can ever impute the shortcoming and transgression of a neighbor to ignorance and
unwatchfulness on his part. While condemning the error or
the deed, it will pity the subject or the agent. Sensitive to
sin, it will impute the commission to the father of sin, rather
than to the agent in whom its manifestation may have been,
for anything which generally appears at any particular time,
a mere omission. The greater the cunning or the malice
which may be manifested in any individual or collective offence, the more readily it will trace the baleful appearance
to a contrivance and cruelty which are at once infernal and
superhuman. Living and walking " in the spirit," it can ever
find a way to " resist the Devil," † without murmuring at the
formal evil, which Christians are indeed commanded ‡ not to
resist, and with which they cannot stoop to contend, without
breaking the harmony of their lives. Like their divine Master, they feel that they are sent to call sinners to repentance,
and like Him they are therefore content that the tares shall
be mingled with the wheat, until the great harvest-day, when,

* JER. vi. 16.   † JAM. iv. 7.   ‡ MATT. v. 39.
13 *

through the divine blessing on their labors, the wiles of the "enemy" who "hath done this" shall be fully and finally exposed.

The only excuse which any body of men can have for establishing themselves, or for professing themselves to be established, as the custodians of a particular form of religious belief, lies in the presumption that that form is superior to all others, and in a consequent willingness and gladness, if they be not like the Israelites a professedly exclusive sect, to have their standard of truth brought, at once most closely and most publicly, into comparison with all other standards. This is the very work by which all may most effectually "resist the Devil," a work which is capable of enlisting all the powers of their being, and which the Devil, so surely as there is such an entity, strives most anxiously, as a hater of light, to repress. We have a memorable illustration of the neglect of this work in the early annals of one of our chief American cities. We may trust that the descendants of the Puritans are preparing to abandon the theological libertinism which was the natural result of their former ecclesiastical fastidiousness; and the descendants of the Quakers may well profit by the warning of their example, whenever tempted to disparage the views and to repulse the friendly overtures of others, either by sitting in judgment on their motives, or by alike disregarding their motives and their arguments. The Day of days will, we may hope, not then overtake us "as a thief in the night."

ONE.

"Where shall I join, and where divide?"—
  Such query greets the mental ear
Full oft, of him who would decide
  His doubtful steps by truth severe : —

"Such kind relations God hath made,
  In things with life and things without,
To bless the soul whose course is laid
  Always by Wisdom's secret route ;

"Such harsh exceptions doth ordain,
  To cheat, in circumstances same,
The eager grasp which else would gain
  That wisdom-fruit in folly's name ;

"With such diversity perplexed,
  In all my plans and all my dreams,
How shall I win the prize annexed
  To truthful life and truthful schemes?"

. Find, anxious soul ! thyself within,
  The true diversity and strife :
Fight ever there the king of sin
  With armor of the King of Life.

There seek the pulse of harmony
  Which nurses health, and strength, and joy ;
There shun the jarring mockery
  Which animates but to annoy.

So mayst thou ever learn to sing
  The universal bridal song,
"There's unity in everything,
  Except between the right and wrong."

THE REALIZATION OF REST.

· "They entered not in, because of unbelief."—HEB. iv. 6.

THE right or privilege of rest, even in this world, implies both the duty and the power of rest. As in every other item of man's probational experience, a trinity of principles is here traceable. The austere extreme of duty is connected with the genial and otherwise relaxing one of pleasure by the efficient mean of power. The thing is simpler than the expression; but the expression, if at all intelligible, is worthy of attention on account of its extended applicability. The very same fusion of duty, right, and power is equally observable even in the seemingly antipodal subject of labor. Only when labor and rest shall become indistinguishable by the completion of the probational life, can this trinity, with every other, be lost in the fulfillment of an ideal unity.

Realization, being simply the conversion of the possible into the actual, is only limited, in things possible, by the limitation of human faith in the wisdom of God. However the partial prevalence of evil may bound or qualify our conception of the omnipotence of God, all experience testifies both that he is omniscient, and that his power is not only supreme over all his own undoubted works, but that it is, historically at least, a progressive power. Where the realization, even by faith, of the presence and guidance of such a Being is possible, premeditation on the part of fallible man is obvious insolence. Whatever be the task of any who can be said to have any remaining capacity for service, "that which may be known of God is manifest in them," and becomes at once their law of labor and their hope of rest. This is the true Gospel (Rom. i. 16, 17) wherein, as it is accepted and adhered to, " the righteousness of God," Christ within, " the hope of glory" (1 Cor. i. 30 ; Col. i. 27) is " revealed from faith to faith." The perfect realization of rest by all men, is thus simply conditioned upon their so making their wills a part of the divine will, as that their work shall become a part of the divine work, and their whole life a part of the divine harmony. The extravagances of false metaphysics, to which all prevailing discords and hardships are, openly or secretly, directly traceable (Prov. xxi. 2), are themselves secondary and not primary evils, being consequential, not causative, to the pride of self-will, and the want of heart-belief.

MUSIC.

From order, the first law of nature,*
  And measure, the mother of art,
Springs the statute of life-legislature,
  That music in life shall have part.

Thus, music's a current compelling
  As gently possessed in its source ;
Or, as oceanward leaping and swelling,
  It channels our life in its course.

True music corrects all distortions,
  Disgusting, deluding, or droll,
By supplying, in proper proportions,
  The mixture of senses and soul.

As life settles down in sensation,
  Things present and tangible rule,
And the glories of inner creation
  Recede from the thought of the fool.

Let music, with clamor diluted,
  Be poured in his wondering ear,
And the cure to the case may be suited,
  And Orphic enchantments appear.

As rises the soul in dominion
  O'er art, and o'er nature as curst,
It will hardly depress its free pinion
  So basely to quench its pure thirst.

For music remains, in its essence,
  The concert of nature and mind,
Which foretokens the rich coalescence
  In heaven reserved for mankind.

* "The one underlying postulate of all science is the harmony of Truth with itself."—
North American Review, XCIX. 404.

THE NEW YEAR.

"The times of this ignorance God winked at; but now commandeth all men everywhere to repent."—ACTS xvii. 30.

AS change and time are inseparable elements of individual experience, so revolution and progress are allied facts, by which the guidance of Divine Providence is manifested in the collective history of mankind. As the phenomena of physical life are found to be maintained only at the expense of a continual death of the constituent parts of living organisms, and as the lapse of time itself is known only by the changes which we are in the habit of imputing to its agency, so do we find all social progress to depend upon gradual but continual destruction and reconstruction of outward institutions. What time and progress and vitality essentially are, we need not expect availingly to know, until our eyes may be opened to behold the realities of eternity, as our feet become planted upon the immutable foundation, which, through the mercy of God in Christ Jesus, has been laid in Zion, as a refuge from the fatal ravages of sin. When the last times shall indeed have passed over us, and the company of the redeemed shall realize that "as in Adam all died, so in Christ all are made alive," the earth will doubtless be released from the participation in its master's curse, which has been expressly recorded for our instruction. Without vainly undertaking to speculate upon the crowning changes, physical and spiritual, which will usher in that Divine order of things, we may safely assume that revolution and progress, if they shall then survive, will be nothing more or less than the working and expression of an unwasting and ever expanding state of perfection. The curtain of futurity will then, indeed, be withdrawn, and a new era of everlasting happiness dawn upon all who shall have walked by the true faith, and held fast the true hope, and pursued the true love through the darkness, and dangers, and conflicts of time.

This great revolution is certainly the one event which .'e-mands our constant attention over and through all particular changes, being that to which they are all tributary as parts of a whole. Such particular changes, therefore, as are obviously typical of that general one, become especially interesting to us as natural mementoes of that of which we have but too much need to be reminded. The rotation of the seasons is an impressive emblem of the ever moving, and yet ever restricted and ever recurring variety of human experience, as developed in the history, either of individual or of social life. The era, therefore, arbitrary as it must be, at which we agree for the sake of uniformity to compute that a new year has commenced its course, is one full of profitable suggestion to the reflective mind. As accountable and fallible beings, we then seem to be especially called upon to review and correct our accounts, in anticipation of that final settlement, at which " the Judge of all the earth" will preside, and to which all nations and generations of men will be witnesses.

The contemplation of that awfully grand and surely impending event, is well fitted to impress us all deeply with the conviction that our destination, like our origin, is, so far, one. In the blindness of self-conceit, and in the distracting idolatry of diverse lusts, we are indeed prone to forget the filial and fraternal ties of duty, and to seek to carve out a career of individual independence, even " as gods, knowing good and evil" for ourselves, and using the gifts of creation as in our own right, and for the purpose of private pleasure, profit, or glory. Hence alienations, divisions, discords, and at last open fightings, inevitably ensue. The charity, or love, which "begins at home," and which is born of faith, and nourished by hope, is the only effectual antidote to this insinuating and deceptive poison of selfishness. As that Divine grace finds place in our hearts, we will neither seek nor wish for any separation from our fellow-beings, short of that in which all our differences and all our agreements will be for ever absorbed, when the " Son of man" shall separate the souls of all nations, "one from another, as a shepherd divideth his sheep from the goats."

The condition of a community being merely the reflected aggregate and average of the individuals composing it, public events may often be prudently regarded as the evidence of tendencies in private practice which may have been previously unsuspected. In the confusion which now so conspicuously prevails in the church and in the world, can we not discover a warning to enter into the closet of our own hearts, and examine into the state of the account, by which we may "know our own selves" by the aid of Him who "is in us, except we be reprobates?" Head-work may guide our hands into a plausible conformity with the labors and views of our fellow-men ; but heart-work alone can guide both our heads and our hands in harmonious obedience to the pure and progressive dictates of Truth. May the New Year indeed become the herald of the ever new and Divine order in which a just subordination and a true co-operation shall increasingly triumph over the hostile influence of confusion and competition, however speciously these may be often disguised as promoters of peace and prosperity !

1st Mo. 1863.

14

TIME AND ETERNITY.

TIME'S level stretch as measured by the years,.
History scans, and her memento rears.
Eternity rolls on in state sublime,
Although by men misnamed the flight of time.
Not flight, but tarriance, is of time the woe;
Not real progress, but deceitful show,
If men rise not eternity to know.
Varied in vastness with his mental reach,
Eternity shines through the life of each,
Revealing all which time appears to teach.
Soul is the seat of wisdom. To its Source
Aspire in prayer with all thy private force,
Requesting thence to be instructed how
Years endless roll in the ETERNAL NOW!

AFTER-THOUGHT.

"Other foundation can no man lay than that is laid."—1 Cor. iii. 11.

"True philosophy will often have occasion to show that supposed problems are no problems at all, but mere impositions of the mind upon itself, arising out of its unrectified position—errors grounded upon errors. A much better test of a sound philosophy than the number of pre-existing problems which it solves, will be the quality of those which it proposes. By raising the station of the spectator it will bring a region of new inquiry within his view; and the very faculty of comprehending these questions will often depend upon the station from which they are viewed."—De Quincey.

DESIRING to attain to all possible explicitness of statement, without pretending to disguise the fragmentary and too disjointed nature of his views of Truth, the author cannot conclude his labor of literary patch-work without endeavoring to add to its coherency, by anticipating probable and perhaps plausible objections. He deems it prudent to disclaim all definitive recognition both of the fundamental duality of Manes and of the fundamental unity of Hegel. He deems it alike unnecessary to begin with the one by cutting the Gordian Knot of the problem of Evil; and with the other, by assuming an ambiguous paradox (the identity of Being and Nothing), to which all minor diversities of view shall be systematically subordinated. He would rather content himself with simply forewarning the inexperienced inquirer, of the danger, ever imminent in proportion as his sphere of knowledge or experience shall be a limited one, of mistaking mere opposition, or antithesis of view, for actual

14

contradiction, or incongruity of fact. With that expansion of consciousness, which ever attends the life of true feeling, earnest thinking and faithful working, the very centre of consciousness, or the intellectual stand-point, is gradually corrected, so that views which at first seemed wholly antipodal may at last be found to be really, closely as well as harmoniously related. Through all degrees of fragmentary attainment, it is thus evident, subjective truth or the truth of individual perception, can be no sure test of objective truth or the truth of catholic reality; so that the most fundamental questions are most wisely left undecided, their premature decision, overt or covert, inevitably entailing misapprehension and discord. Until the realization of that life of perfect unity in which the natural antithesis of matter and spirit * shall be found to have been a merely subjective phenomenon, this universal though individual antithesis must, with its accompanying power of synthesis,† present to each individual his own several triune law of work. Like the unswerving living and seeing wheels of the prophet's vision,‡ these laws in their practical application and progressive revolution, will be incapable of clashing together, or of at all differing except by including or being included in one another; thus demonstrating that in the principle of Trinity lies the largest law of probationary Humanity—Man's sole refuge from the present distractions of a fallen Duality, and his sole hope of the ultimate realization of a divine Unity.

* "Twain extremes," p. 159.   † "Centric mean," p. 159.
‡ Ezek., ch. i., &c.

TRINITY.

THE mystery of one and three
  Is that which meets us ever,
A lock and key which aye agree,
  And yield to wise endeavor.

From twain extremes on centric mean
  In common cause revolving,
O'er life's dark dreams a light is seen
  The shades of doubt dissolving.

On living wheels with eyes begirt
  Creation still is moving:
Through death's dread seals life leaps alert,
  A Maker's might still proving.

So heaven and hell, o'er-spreading all
  The field of man's probation,
The doctrine tell of Adam's fall,
  And of the great salvation.

Their germs pervade all charms that lure
  Our passions or our senses;
And, as obeyed, our bliss ensure,
  Or punish our offences.

May all we see, and all we do,
  Illustrate and inherit
The knowledge free and profit true,
  Which turn on God's good Spirit!

By faith death's sting alive to shun,
  We then the grace shall gather
In every thing* to know the Son,
  And, through the Son, the Father.

    * "In him all things consist." COL. i. 17.

www.ingramcontent.com/pod-product-compliance
Lightning Source LLC
Chambersburg PA
CBHW021108020726
47500CB00003B/660